GOD'S WORD B.C.

by

John W. Wade

You may obtain a 64-page leader's guide to accompany this paperback. Order number 41021 from Standard Publishing or your local supplier.

A Division of Standard Publishing
Cincinnati, Ohio 45231
No. 41020

Library of Congress Cataloging in Publication Data

Wade, John William, 1924-
  God's word B.C.

    1. Bible. O.T.—History of Biblical events.
I. Title. II. Title: God's word B.C.
BS1197.W325 1983   221.9'5   83-349
ISBN 0-87239-667-3

Printed in U.S.A.   1983

Table of Contents

Foreword

Many Christians have a hangup about the Old Testament. For them, it is a book of hard-to-pronounce names and strange customs. Or worse, it is a book of mystery because for all practical purposes it is a closed book, unknown and unstudied. How unfortunate that such attitudes have robbed us of the blessings that can come from the study of these thirty-nine books we call the Old Testament!

There are several good reasons for studying the Old Testament.

1. First of all, it is a part of God's Holy Word, inspired just as the New Testament is. This reason alone makes it a subject worthy of our prayerful and careful study.

2. The Old Testament is also valuable as a source of knowledge about our spiritual roots. Christianity was not just suddenly dropped upon the human race without any prior announcement or advance preparation. Knowing one's roots helps a person gain a sense of identity and establish a sense of destiny.

3. A knowledge of the Old Testament is absolutely essential if one is to understand the New Testament. Someone has aptly stated, "The Old Testament is the New Testament concealed; the New Testament is the Old Testament revealed." Just as one would not attempt to learn calculus without first acquiring a basic understanding of arithmetic, so to understand and appreciate the New Testament we need some knowledge of the Old.

4. Jesus frequently quoted the Old Testament as proof of His messiahship. Paul and the other New Testament writers also made many references to the Old Testament. One of the most striking proofs of the inspiration of the Scriptures is the fulfilled prophecies of the Old Testament.

5. The Old Testament contains accounts of the lives of many people. These accounts can be a source of help to Christians. We can learn to avoid the mistakes of those people and emulate their faith and courage.

6. One other reason for studying the Old Testament, and a most important one at that, is that a knowledge of the Old Testament is necessary if we are to understand God's unfolding plan for human redemption. Even before the foundations of the world were laid, God had made provision for man's redemption. With

man's fall in the Garden of Eden, that plan was put into operation. All through the Old Testament and then the New, we see it unfolding until it reaches its culminating victory in Revelation.

Admittedly, studying the Old Testament is not easy. Like every study worth the effort, it does take some work and concentration. We hope the brief introduction contained in this book will encourage you to undertake further study and will provide a few helps for you to use along the way.

In this study we have used the *New International Version* for all quotations except where noted otherwise. This widely available translation provides a good, readable, modern English text for the Old Testament.

In the Beginning

Genesis 1—3

"In the beginning God"—thus with sublime simplicity the book of Genesis begins. Without resorting to speculation or delving into metaphysics, the writer of Genesis sets forth the facts of creation. In the strictest sense this account is not science, since science depends upon phenomena that can be observed, measured, and repeated. Nor is it history, for history is based upon various kinds of records left by those who have observed the events in question. It certainly is not myth, because myth is shot through with absurdities and strange creations of the human imagination. One has to study only briefly some of the pagan accounts of creation to realize how different they are from Genesis.

If the Genesis account is not science, not history, and not myth, what is it? Obviously, it is revelation. Since there were no eyewitnesses to these events, the information had to come to Moses by divine revelation. In revealing information to man, God has always acted sparingly, never divulging more than was necessary to accomplish His purpose. Thus it should not surprise us that Genesis is a very abbreviated account of creation.

I. God, the Creator *(Genesis 1:1–2:25)*

Modern scientists grapple with the origins of our physical universe. The most popular theory among scientists today has been dubbed the "big bang" theory. According to this theory our universe began billions of years ago in a mighty cosmic explosion that sent matter and energy hurling across the vast reaches of space. But this theory still leaves unexplained the origin of physical matter, the atomic and subatomic particles that make up the stuff of the universe.

The Bible goes behind all these speculations, interesting as they are, to the real beginning when nothing existed but God. Since God is a Spirit and not physical, we do not have to theorize about His beginning. He has always existed. Out of His vast power He spoke the heavens and the earth into existence, not from some pre-existing matter, but from nothing.

A. Creator of the Physical Universe

First He created the physical universe. This creative process proceeded in an orderly fashion. The earth as originally created was dark, formless, and empty. Then into this primal chaos God sent light, separating it from the darkness, thus ending the first day of creation (Genesis 1:1-5).

This raises an interesting and somewhat controversial issue. What is meant here by the term *day?* (verse 5). Some hold that it means a literal twenty-four hour day like today or yesterday. Others take the position that the word refers to a long period during which God carried out His creative activity. The Scriptures afford many examples in which this term is used in a figurative rather than literal sense to mean a longer period of time. Taking the word *day* here to mean a long period of time does have the advantage of providing a more convenient explanation for the geological record we see about us. Persons who hold this view are not necessarily committed to a belief in organic evolution.

On the second day the clouds were lifted from the earth, providing the expanse of sky with watery clouds above it and the waters of the earth below it (Genesis 1:6-8).

On the third day the continents and islands emerged from the sea to provide dry land (Genesis 1:9, 10). These conditions allowed the first forms of life—plant life—to appear. The origin of life is the second great mystery that modern scientists have not been able to explain. They have advanced all kinds of interesting theories about how certain conditions produced life spontaneously. Yet in spite of all their efforts, men have never been able to produce life from lifeless matter.

8

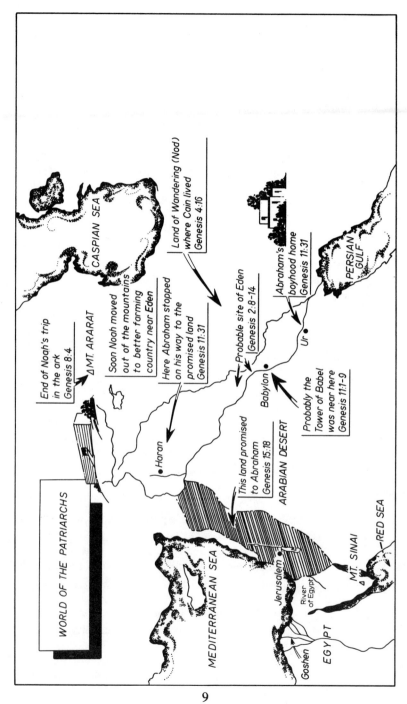

WORLD OF THE PATRIARCHS

End of Noah's trip in the ark
Genesis 8:4

△MT. ARARAT

CASPIAN SEA

Soon Noah moved out of the mountains to better farming country near Eden

Land of Wandering (Nod) where Cain lived
Genesis 4:16

Here Abraham stopped on his way to the promised land
Genesis 11:31

Abraham's boyhood home
Genesis 11:31

PERSIAN GULF

• Haran

Probable site of Eden
Genesis 2:8-14

Ur •

Babylon •

Probably the Tower of Babel was near here
Genesis 11:1-9

ARABIAN DESERT

This land promised to Abraham
Genesis 15:18

MEDITERRANEAN SEA

Jerusalem •

River of Egypt

MT. SINAI △

RED SEA

Goshen

EGYPT

9

Along with the creation of plant life, God established the law that governs it: each plant will reproduce after its own kind (Genesis 1:11-13). It was God's purpose to provide stability in the world He created, and this law helps accomplish that. How chaotic our world would be if we planted wheat that one year produced wheat and the next year thistles, or a fruit tree that gave sweet, nourishing fruit one year and poisonous fruit the next!

On the fourth day God established the heavenly bodies to mark the seasons, days, and years. It would seem that the heavenly bodies had been created earlier, but on the fourth day they were set up as signs to measure the passing of time (Genesis 1:14-19).

B. Creator of Animal Life

On the fifth day God placed animal life upon the earth. First came the "great creatures of the sea and every living and moving thing with which the water teems." We can only guess at the countless thousands of different species that were created. Many of these have long since perished, leaving no trace, or at best, only fragmentary evidence scattered here and there in the rocks. The vast oceans undoubtedly still have many species that man has not seen or catalogued.

Not only was animal life planted in the seas, but the air was populated by various kinds of winged creatures. But God needed to do more than bring them into existence and give them life. He had also to create the proper conditions to sustain life. We are only beginning to realize how fragile life is. It can exist only within a narrow range of temperatures and within a delicately balanced environment. We can but stand in awe of God's omnipotence in planning the universe, creating it, and sustaining it (Genesis 1:20-23).

On the sixth day God created the animals of the earth. Three distinct categories of animals seem to be included: "livestock, creatures that move along the ground, and wild animals." Apparently these categories are intended to be very general and include mammals, reptiles, and even insects (Genesis 1:24, 25).

C. Creator of Man

Finally, to climax His creative activities, God created man "in his own image." No animal in God's creation is so described, clearly indicating that man is unique. Though he shares many qualities with animals, yet man is in this respect, at least, unique.

10

Genesis 1 gives only a very brief account of creation in most general terms. Chapter 2 continues the account, giving more details about man's creation. We are told that he was made from the dust of the earth, God breathing into his nostrils the breath of life after He had shaped him. God then placed him in the Garden of Eden to tend it and to enjoy its fruits. We are not given the exact location of the garden, but the mention of the Tigris and Euphrates Rivers suggests its approximate location (Genesis 2:10-14). Many scholars place it in ancient Mesopotamia, or Iraq, as it is now called.

Because of man's unique relationship to God, God gave him dominion over the animals. Since it was God's intention to place man over the animals, He endowed him with superior intelligence to carry out this mandate. But there was a danger involved in this mandate, the danger that man's dominion would be turned to selfish purposes. In our own times we have seen man become so successful in his contest with the animals that many species have been hunted to extinction and other species are endangered. God certainly never intended that man exercise his power in this ruthless fashion, but once sin entered the world, man threw aside most of his restraints.

It seems clear that from the very beginning God intended for man to work. Many today dream of a place where there will be no work and no responsibilities, supposing this to be some modern Eden. But the original garden, even before the fall, was not such a place. While it is true that the fall made man's labor far more burdensome, yet he had responsibilities even in Eden. God created man with the ability to work and He also gave him the ability to enjoy the fruits of his labor. Is it not altogether possible that much of man's unrest today comes because he has not learned the joys and blessings that honest labor brings?

It was never God's intention that man be alone, and so God created woman as his companion. In the second chapter (verses 21-24) we are told that Eve was created from Adam's rib, indicating their closeness. When God created the human race male and female, He intended a man and a woman to establish a special relationship between themselves. This relationship was to be more powerful than the ties of blood, for God intended that man "leave his father and mother and be united to his wife" (2:24), or to use the familiar language of the King James Version, he was to leave his parents and cleave to his wife. As a result of this leaving

11

and cleaving, the two become "one flesh" in the mystery of the marriage bond. Many modern marriage partners never know the real joys of becoming one flesh because they have never really fully experienced the "leaving" and "cleaving" that God requires.

II. Sin Enters the World *(Genesis 3:1-24)*

Men have wrestled for centuries with the problem of sin and the suffering it brings. Philosophers and theologians have suggested numerous sources for sin, yet none of these suggestions seems to be entirely satisfying. Even the Bible does not give us much information about the origin of sin. Instead, the Scriptures concentrate on how sin affects the human race, and, most importantly, what God has done to save man from the consequences of his sin. Genesis 3 is one of the most important chapters in the Bible in dealing with this problem.

A. Satan Appears on the Scene

We are told nothing about the origin of Satan, but we soon learn something about his intentions. Appearing to Eve in the form of a serpent, he quickly sought to lead her to disobey God's commandment. It is worth noting the process that he used to lead her into that first act of rebellion.

First of all, Satan came to her when she was alone. Persons can certainly be tempted in the company of others. In fact, others may on occasion be used by Satan as a means of temptation. Yet there is strength in numbers, and Satan undoubtedly felt that Eve was more vulnerable alone than when she and Adam were together. It is also likely that we have an abbreviated version of the temptation and that this was not the first time he had appeared to her. A person seldom succumbs to Satan's blandishments the first time he offers them; and he, knowing our nature even better than we, is quite willing to be patient and come back again and again until we surrender. Alexander Pope said it well in his lines:

> Vice is a monster of so frightful mien,
> As to be hated needs but to be seen;
> Yet seen too oft, familiar with her face,
> We first endure, then pity, then embrace.

Satan's next ploy was to arouse within her a sense of restraint,

12

a feeling that she was being denied something that rightfully belonged to her. "Did God really say, 'You must not eat from any tree in the garden'?" asked the serpent. His purpose, of course, was to make God appear unjust. It is amazing how easily the tempter can get us to covet the one thing we don't have and, in the midst of plenty, don't need. Certainly the forbidden fruit was not necessary for Adam and Eve in the garden where they had all kinds of fruit to choose from. Yet Eve was led to desire it precisely because it was forbidden.

The next step in Satan's plan was to make God out a liar. God had decreed that Adam and Eve would die if they touched the fruit. "You will not surely die," responded the serpent. Quite obviously either God or Satan was lying, but by this time Eve was so desirous of the fruit that she was ready to believe Satan's lie.

Satan's next lie was to make it appear that the real reason God denied them the fruit was that He was jealous. Eating the fruit would allow them to be like God, he said, and God would do anything to prevent that. As preposterous as this lie was, Satan made it sound reasonable to the woman, and she believed it. If we have difficulty understanding how anyone could be so foolish, we need only look around and see some of the lies that Satan uses today.

Satan climaxed his efforts by leading Eve to see how attractive the fruit was. Not only would the fruit provide physical food, it would also bring sensual pleasure. More than that, it would feed spiritual pride by imparting wisdom. This suggests at least three avenues through which temptations come, a suggestion that finds a parallel in 1 John 2:16.

Satan's cunning and perseverance prevailed, and Eve ate of the fruit. Her immediate response must have been one of pleasure and perhaps a bit of relief because she didn't drop dead. This latter fact must have reassured her that Satan was indeed telling the truth and that God had lied about the deadly qualities. Thus reassured, she offered the fruit to Adam.

B. Adam's Sin

Why did Adam accept the fruit? He had not been conditioned by Satan's hard sell as had Eve. Paul suggests that Adam was not deceived as was Eve, but entered into sin with full knowledge of what he was doing (1 Timothy 2:14), enticed by his love for Eve. Milton in *Paradise Lost* expresses this view as he has Adam say:

How can I live without thee? how forgo
Thy sweet converse and love so dearly joined,
To live again in these wild woods forlorn?
Should God create another Eve, and I
Another rib afford, yet loss of thee
Would never from my heart. No, no! I feel
The link of nature draw me: flesh of flesh,
Bone of my bone thou art, and from thy state
Mine never shall be parted, bliss or woe.

C. Consequence of Their Sin

When sin entered the world, far-reaching consequences soon followed. The law of the harvest—as a man soweth, so shall he reap—applies in the spiritual realm as well as the physical. In this case the harvest was a bitter one.

Perhaps the first and immediate result of the disobedience was that man felt alienated from God. Sin created a barrier, a sense of shame and guilt that caused Adam to hide when God came seeking him in the cool of the evening. Time has not changed this fact. Sin still alienates man from God and leaves man with a sense of shame.

Second, death entered the world. Now it is true that Adam and Eve did not drop dead the instant they tasted the fruit, but from that moment they began to die. It was only a matter of time until death came in full force. They did, however, die spiritually the moment they sinned. Sin separates man from God, which is what spiritual death really is. A greater tragedy was that the penalty of physical death passed on to every descendant of the first pair. Further, spiritual death is the lot of everyone who sins as did Adam and Eve.

Another tragic result was that Adam and Eve lost their blessed home in Eden. They could no longer live there lest they eat of the tree of life and live forever. Nothing could be more painful than living forever in a sinful state, and so their expulsion from the garden was, in a sense, an act of mercy. Driven from the garden, they had to make their way in a world that was no longer friendly. The ground would produce thorns and thistles instead of delectable fruit, and much labor would be required for man to grow a crop. To make sure they would not return, cherubim and a flaming sword stood guard over the way to the tree of life. Thus our first parents learned that crime does not pay.

D. A Gleam in the Dark

It would be difficult to imagine a more dismal scene than that of Adam and Eve making their way from the garden with heavy hearts and leaden feet. Milton concludes his great epic with these words:

They hand in hand with wandering steps and slow,
Through Eden took their solitary way.

But as dark as this scene was, a gleam of hope shone through. Man's state was not to be one of total misery without hope. God pronounced a curse upon the serpent and then added a prophecy:

And I will put enmity between you and the woman, and between your offspring and hers; he will crush your head, and you will strike his heel.

Here in veiled words was God's promise that He would through the offspring of the woman—Christ—crush the head of the serpent. Christ's sacrificial death on the cross would provide the blow to crush Satan, to burst the shackles of death he had thrown about man. At the same time, the ominous word that the serpent would strike the heel of woman's offspring points to His painful death on the cross.

Conclusion

In three short chapters we are given a brief outline of creation. It is significant that after each act of creation God pronounced His blessing upon it—"God saw that it was good." Such a divine evaluation should prevent our ever rejecting any part of God's creation as dirty or evil. Finally, God made man "in his own image." God pronounced an even greater blessing on this concluding act of creation—"It was very good."

Yet into this blessed creation came sin, with all its damning, blighting curse. It shattered the bliss that God had intended for Eden and sent man into a hostile world. Yet it was not a future without hope, for God had made provision for man's restoration by planning to send His own Son to be our Redeemer.

After the Fall

Genesis 4:1—11:9

I. Adam and Eve Begin Life Outside the Garden

Eden was forever closed to Adam and Eve. Remorse must have flooded their hearts when the realization finally sank in that they could not go back again. There was nothing for them to do but to make the best of the situation.

A. Two Sons Are Born *(Genesis 4:1-5)*

Soon a son, Cain, was born to them. Like every parent, they must have had high hopes for him at his birth. Since God had promised that the seed of the woman would eventually bruise the head of the serpent, they may have felt that Cain was the fulfillment of that promise. Little did they know that generations must pass before God would finally complete this promise by sending His own Son.

Before long another son, Abel, arrived. This, too, must have brought rejoicing to Adam and Eve. But jealousy on the part of Cain eventually turned this joy to tragedy. The Scriptures, as is so often the case in these early chapters of Genesis, probably give us an abbreviated account of the rivalry that led to murder. It seems altogether likely that there were many other incidents that gradually resulted in Cain's explosive violence. Satan undoubtedly was at work on Cain just as he had worked on his parents.

People do not often become bad suddenly. The deterioration of character, just as the development of character, is usually a slow, gradual process. Sometimes it even proceeds so gradually that we are not aware of it either in others or in ourselves.

B. Violence in the Family *(Genesis 4:6-12)*

The event that triggered Cain's violence was their bringing offerings to the Lord. We know very little about the offerings they brought or why they brought them. Hebrews 11:4 tells us that "by faith Abel offered God a better sacrifice than Cain did," and so it seems reasonable to assume that God had commanded them to make an offering. We are not told why God was pleased with Abel's offering but displeased with Cain's. Some hold that the difference lay in the fact that Abel made an offering of animals while Cain brought fruits of the soil. But this scarcely seems an adequate reason, because later on, under the Mosaic code, grain and other fruits were acceptable.

Probably the real cause of God's rejection was that Cain's attitude was wrong. Perhaps he brought his offering with a stingy and resentful heart. It is clear from the actions that followed that he had a jealous heart. Cain did not realize or had not learned that God is not nearly as interested in externals as He is in the condition of one's heart.

As a result of God's rejection of his offering, Cain became quite angry, so angry that it showed plainly in his face. God assured Cain that the solution to his problem was quite simple. All Cain had to do to gain God's approval was to follow God's commandments. But this, unfortunately, he was not willing to do. Instead of facing up to his failures, he sought to blame everyone but himself. The Scriptures describe his temptation in interesting terms: "sin is crouching at the door." Sin is depicted as an animal about to pounce upon its prey, language suggestive of 1 Peter 5:8 that describes the devil as a roaring lion seeking whom he may devour. But Cain was not yet at that moment a helpless victim ready to be consumed by sin. He could resist, for he had it within his power to master the temptation. Cain, like many persons today, was ready to give in to sin without a struggle.

And give in he did in a most vicious way. The New International Version, differing from the King James in 4:8, indicates that Cain deliberately enticed his brother out into the field where he could attack him. Thus his action was calculated, cold-blooded

17

murder, not an act of violence stemming from momentary anger. We are not told what efforts Cain made to conceal his crime, but he failed. No effort to hide murder could conceal the fact from God.

Cain's first response was to disavow any responsibility for his brother. Men ever since have been shrugging off their duties to those about them by asking, "Am I my brother's keeper?" This is the bartender's out when he sells his poisonous drink. It may be used by parents to excuse the neglect of their children, or by Christians when they avoid their opportunities for evangelism. But in every case the answer is the same—yes!

C. Cain's Punishment *(Genesis 4:13-24)*

As a punishment Cain was to find the soil unproductive, and he was to become a wanderer on the face of the earth. His first fear was that he would be killed by whoever met him, but to avoid this God placed a mark upon him. Scholars have speculated about what this mark was, but the Scriptures do not tell us. Cain was forced to leave the pleasant surroundings near Eden and flee to the land of Nod, somewhere to the east of Eden.

The verses that follow tell of some of the descendants of Cain. It is a tragic fact that the sins of the fathers are often visited upon the children. This was certainly true in the case of Cain's descendants. Their lives often reflected the violence and worldliness he had shown in his life. What he had sown, the world had to reap.

D. The Birth of Seth *(Genesis 4:25–5:32)*

It was God's plan to send a Redeemer for the human race through the lineage of Adam; but with Abel murdered and Cain a renegade, God's plan seemed thwarted. But not for long, for God gave Adam and Eve another son, Seth. This son was destined to become the ancestor of Noah, who was born many centuries later. Between Seth and Noah were several outstanding men, including Enoch, who did not die but in some miraculous way was taken by God (5:24), and Methuselah, whose longevity record of 969 years has never been surpassed.

II. The Flood *(Genesis 6:1–9:17)*

At a few points in history, the whole course of human experience has been changed and given a radical new direction. The flood was certainly one of those history-changing events.

18

A. The Growing Wickedness of Man

In the period from Adam to Noah the human population expanded rapidly. The fact that people lived to very great ages, giving the women long bearing periods, contributed greatly to this population explosion. It was God's purpose that the human race should people the earth, and this commandment man faithfully carried out.

But along with the growth in numbers was a corresponding growth in wickedness, certainly not a part of God's plan. Man became so thoroughly immersed in sin that "every inclination of the thoughts of his heart was only evil all the time" (6:5). We like to believe that in every person is a little spark of decency, a spark that under proper circumstances may be kindled into a glowing light. But this belief may be a rather naive sentimentality, for at least at the point in history described here such was not the case. Men had become so wicked that "the Lord was grieved that he had made man."

The God who is completely holy found this situation intolerable. Man must be destroyed. God is a God of love, but He is also a God of righteousness. Let those who think Jehovah God to be a benign and sentimental old grandfather take heed. He will not tolerate sin forever.

B. God Uses Noah

But even as God prepared to send His righteous judgment upon a wicked world, His mercy intervened to save one righteous man and his family. It seems incredible that, in all the vast multitudes, this one man remained true to God. We wish we knew more about Noah. How did he learn about God? What factors in his character kept him faithful when all about had rejected God?

God's judgment upon the world was to be a vast flood of unprecedented proportions. We are not told why God chose this method to bring judgment, but we must accept by faith that it was the most appropriate method. Water does suggest a certain cleansing quality that was needed then.

We may also ask why God instructed Noah to build an ark as a means of escape. Certainly God could have sent angels to deliver Noah and his family. Perhaps God was suggesting to future generations that while in one sense man is saved by God's grace, yet in another sense man is expected to put in some effort to gain his salvation.

God's instructions for building the ark were very precise. He specified the size (approximately 450 feet long, 75 feet wide, and 45 feet high). This would be a good sized vessel even today, but it needed to be large because it had to provide space for two of each of the unclean animals and seven, or seven pairs, of each of the clean animals (7:2), plus all the food this menagerie would consume in a year's time.

We can only marvel at Noah's courage and energy as he undertook this mammoth task. He probably had little help beyond the members of his own family. Indeed, his neighbors probably looked upon his efforts with derision, even questioning his sanity for building such a boat so far from water. But Noah did not spend all his time building the ark; some of it he spent preaching. (See 1 Peter 3:18-20; 2 Peter 2:5.) If we are correct in supposing that God first revealed His judgment a hundred and twenty years before the flood (6:3), then Noah had this period to carry out his preaching while he continued to build the ark, a gigantic object lesson for all to see.

C. The Coming of the Flood

The day finally came in Noah's six hundredth year when the ark was completed and God was ready to execute His judgment. The animals were gathered aboard the ark, and Noah and his family—his wife, his three sons, and their wives—went aboard. "Then the Lord shut him in" (7:16). What a ring of finality these words have! Up until that very moment men and women might have repented and found safety aboard the ark. But once that door was closed, it was too late. Jesus reminds us that His return will come just as unexpectedly and with similar finality (Matthew 24:36-41).

For forty days and nights the rains came, but in addition, the "springs of the great deep burst forth" (7:11), possibly indicating great geological shifts that enhanced the destructive volume and power of the flood waters. Total destruction swept across the earth. It is disturbing to realize that not only were the wicked destroyed but that many innocent babies and small children perished also. This gives an agonizing illustration of the fact that one of the most terrible things about sin is that it brings suffering not only to the guilty but to the innocent as well.

After Noah and his family had spent approximately a year in the ark, the flood receded and the land dried up sufficiently for them to disembark. We can scarcely imagine their joy as they once again set foot on dry land. It is not surprising, then, that one of the first things Noah did was to build an altar upon which he offered sacrifices to the Lord. A heart that recognizes God as the source of blessing is a heart that finds joy in worshipful praise of God.

D. God's Covenant With Noah

In every age God has dealt with man upon the basis of an agreement or covenant. Since the emergence of Noah from the ark signaled the beginning of a new era, it was appropriate that it should be begun with a new covenant. The terms of the covenant were rather general. Man had the duty to repopulate the earth. He was permitted to use both plants and animals for food, avoiding only meat that contained blood. Man was also to refrain from taking human life. Life was considered so precious that murder was to be punished by the execution of the murderer (9:5, 6).

God on His part assured man that he would have dominion over the animals. God also pledged that never again would He send a great flood to destroy the human race. God used the rainbow in the sky as a recurring reminder of this promise.

III. After the Flood *(9:18–11:9)*

A. Noah's Mistake

The closing verses of chapter 9 end on a tragic note. Following the flood, Noah turned to farming for his livelihood. From some of the grapes he grew he made wine. Drinking some of it, he became intoxicated. Perhaps his intoxication was accidental, for the Scriptures do not condemn him for it. But his son, Ham, brought a severe condemnation upon himself because in viewing his father in his nakedness he arrogantly violated an important taboo. As a result of Ham's sin, a curse fell upon his son Canaan, whose descendants were to become the slaves of the descendants of Noah's other two sons, Japheth and Shem.

B. The Tower of Babel

Following the flood, the descendants of Noah settled in the plain of Shinar, which is located in the eastern part of Mesopotamia. They soon hit upon an ambitious plan—they would build a huge tower that would reach to heaven. By so doing they hoped to make a great name for themselves and keep from being "scattered over the face of the whole earth." By desiring a great name for themselves, they were guilty of sinful pride, and by refusing to spread to other places on the earth, they were refusing to obey God's direct commandment to "be fruitful and increase in number and fill the earth" (9:1).

God did not need to take violent measures to solve the problem. All He had to do was to confound their languages. This simple expedient had two results. It stopped their work on the tower at once. Since they could not communicate with one another, they could not coordinate their building efforts. The second result was that their inability to communicate soon forced them to scatter. Living in a close community requires a certain level of communication. When this is lacking, misunderstanding, disagreement, and violence soon follow.

Just how many different languages God imposed upon them we do not know. A few would be enough to accomplish His purpose. We need not suppose that the thousands of languages and dialects spoken in the world today all had their origins at the tower of Babel. Certainly most of these developed much later.

Lives of the Patriarchs

Genesis 11:27—50:26

The closing verses of Genesis 11 introduce us to Terah and his sons—Abram, Nahor, and Haran—who then lived in Ur of the Chaldeans. From this point on, the book of Genesis concentrates on Abram and his descendants, for it was through them that God began to reveal His new covenant.

I. Abraham

A. Abram's Call *(Genesis 11:31–12:3)*

While Abram was still living in Ur, God called him to leave and go to a land that God would later reveal to him. (See Acts 7:2, 3.) The writer of the epistle to the Hebrews tells us that by faith Abram was obedient to this commandment. It was indeed an act of faith, for in the first place, he was traveling without a road map or a specific destination. It was also an act of faith because Abram left a comfortable existence in Ur to become a wanderer. Archaeologists have uncovered evidence that Ur enjoyed a high level of culture about 2000 B.C., when Abram lived there.

Archaeologists have also discovered evidence that the people of Ur were polytheists, worshiping many gods. Much of the worship was debased and immoral. We can readily see why God wanted to remove Abram from that kind of an environment. We are not told how Abram had remained a follower of the true God

23

in the midst of paganism, but apparently this faith had been handed down in his family from Noah. Because this faith had been sustained, God was able to use Abram.

In making his way to the land of promise, Abram, along with his father, Terah, his nephew, Lot, and his wife, Sarai, traveled up the Euphrates River and stopped at Haran. It was here that Terah died at the age of two hundred five. Then probably God once more spoke to Abram, instructing him that it was time to move on to a land God would show him. Even though he was seventy-five years old at the time, Abram did not hesitate to heed God's call. He left Haran for Canaan, where he became a nomad, following his flocks in search of pasture (Genesis 12:4-9).

B. Abraham the Wanderer *(Genesis 12:10–16:16)*
A famine drove him into Egypt, where, even though he conducted himself dishonorably (Genesis 12:14-20), his fortune was

---

Early Old Testament History

Period of Beginnings
Creation
Sin
Flood
Tower of Babel

Dates of these events are not fixed.

Period of Patriarchs
Abraham, Job
Isaac
Jacob
Joseph

About 2000 B.C.

To Egypt and Back
Bondage in Egypt
Exodus
Wandering
Conquest of Canaan
Last Years of Joshua

About 1447 B.C.

---

enhanced. Returning to Canaan, he soon had to settle a dispute between his herdsmen and those of Lot. Abram magnanimously gave Lot the first choice of areas in which to live. Lot chose the well-watered plain of the Jordan, leaving the less desirable hill country to Abram. But Lot's choice proved to be a disastrous one, for eventually he became a resident of the city of Sodom, notorious for its wickedness.

Chapter 14 relates how Abram and his allies had to rescue Lot and his family, who had been taken captive by a marauding band. Returning with the spoils of victory, Abram was met by Melchizedek, the king of Salem (14:18). After he had pronounced a blessing upon Abram, Abram gave his tithe, a tenth, of all the spoils.

Chapter 15 records that God in a vision reassured Abram that He would protect him and give to his descendants all the land stretching from the river of Egypt to the Euphrates. Chapter 16 tells how Sarai, having abandoned hope that she would ever bear Abram a child, gave him her handmaid, Hagar. Hagar bore Abram a son, Ishmael, but he was not the son of promise. Even before his birth God told Hagar that he would be a "wild donkey of a man . . . he will live in hostility toward all his brothers." We can see evidence of that hostility even to this day.

C. Abraham, a Man of Faith *(Genesis 17:1–22:19)*

When Abram was ninety-nine years old, God reaffirmed His covenant with him (Genesis 17:1-27). God promised to bless him and make him the father of many nations. As a symbol of this promised blessing, God changed his name from Abram (meaning "exalted father") to Abraham (meaning "father of many nations"). Sarai's name was changed to Sarah, which indicates her exalted position as mother of nations (17:16). Further God promised to Abraham and his descendants the land of Palestine, then occupied by many different tribes. Through Abraham, God would bless the whole world, a blessing that was fully realized in the coming of Christ. Across the centuries to come, God would bless those who blessed Abraham and his descendants and curse those who cursed them. (See Genesis 12:3.)

Since Ishmael was not the son of promise, God's covenant with Abraham could be fulfilled only if another son should be born to him. God fulfilled His pledge by giving him and Sarah a son, Isaac, in their old age. It was indeed a miracle, for Abraham was a hundred years old at the time of Isaac's birth, and Sarah was ninety.

But between the time of the promise of the son (Genesis 18:1-15) and his birth (Genesis 21:1-7), we are told of the destruction of Sodom and Gomorrah (Genesis 19:1-29). Only Lot and his two daughters escaped the fiery destruction. This episode is a pointed reminder that God will not forever stay His judgment when a people becomes unspeakably corrupt.

Chapter 22 relates what was probably the greatest test of faith Abraham had to face. He was ordered to sacrifice Isaac as a burnt offering. What a flood of emotions and thoughts must have tumbled through his troubled mind! His faith had been strong enough to believe that God could send him a son in his old age; was it strong enough to offer that son as a sacrifice? The writer of Hebrews assures us that his faith could indeed stand the test: "By faith Abraham, when God tested him, offered Isaac as a sacrifice" (Hebrews 11:17). We are also told the reason for that faith: "Abraham reasoned that God could raise the dead, and figuratively speaking, he did receive Isaac back from death" (Hebrews 11:19). The dramatic conclusion came when God provided a ram for the sacrifice. Abraham had passed the test with flying colors!

II. Isaac

A. The Son of Promise

Compared either to the life of his father Abraham or to the life of his son Jacob, Isaac's life may seem rather quiet and uneventful. As a child of promise in his parents' old age, he must have been given extra protection and every advantage. Yet he gives no evidence of having been spoiled by all of this attention. He was apparently an obedient son, for he was willing to be sacrificed by his father. We need to keep in mind that he was no small boy when this happened, but a young man full of strength and vigor. No doubt he could have overpowered his aged father and escaped from him had he so desired.

B. Isaac Takes a Bride *(Genesis 24)*

He also obediently submitted to his father's desire that he not take a bride from among the Canaanites. The story of how Abraham's servant was sent back to Haran to seek a wife from among the family of Abraham is one of the most delightful in the Old Testament (Genesis 24). One cannot help admiring the courage of the beautiful Rebekah as she left her home for a land she knew nothing about to meet her bridegroom whom she did not know.

To this couple were born twin sons, Jacob and Esau (Genesis 25). Even before their birth it was predicted that "the older will serve the younger." The boys were twins, but Esau was born before Jacob. Since the two developed such different personalities, it would be most surprising if they had not frequently quarreled or even fought as they grew toward maturity. Even the parents became involved in this. Isaac preferred Esau, who was a hunter and outdoorsman, while Rebekah preferred Jacob, who chose to spend much of his time about his mother's tent.

C. Isaac, a Patient Man *(Genesis 26)*

Isaac was a man of gentle patience. When the Philistines stopped up some of the wells his father had dug, he reopened them. His servants later dug a new well, only to have it claimed by the Philistines. Isaac quietly moved on and dug another well. This the Philistines also claimed. Once more he patiently moved on, digging a third well. His patience was finally rewarded, for the Philistines did not claim this third well. God continued to bless Isaac, and he prospered greatly, a fact that was not lost on Abimelech, the Philistine king, who came seeking a peace treaty. As a result, Isaac was able to avoid further conflicts with his neighbors.

But even though Isaac was able to live at peace with his neighbors, all was not well at home. Much to the sorrow of Isaac and Rebekah, Esau chose wives from among the Hittites. The next chapter in this family conflict unfolded when Jacob plotted with his mother to gain Isaac's blessing intended for Esau (Genesis 27). Jacob had earlier taken advantage of Esau to gain his birthright, and so it is not surprising that Esau held a grudge against his brother. He thought he would kill Jacob; but to avoid grieving his father he decided to postpone the murder till the death of the old man (Genesis 27:41).

III. Jacob

Jacob, the third of the patriarchs, certainly seemed the least likely to be used of God. He took advantage of his brother's weakness to gain his birthright and deceived his blind father to gain his blessing. Yet God was able to use him because he did have faith.

27

A. Jacob's Flight *(Genesis 27:41–28:22)*

As a result of Esau's anger, Rebekah felt it best for Jacob to take a prolonged vacation in a distant land—Paddan Aram, to be exact. Even in this matter, Rebekah misrepresented to Isaac the purpose of his leaving, pretending that she wanted him out of Palestine lest he marry a Hittite or Canaanite woman. And so he set out on his long journey, but at Bethel he was brought up short by a dream in which he saw a stairway reaching to Heaven. Above it stood almighty God, who renewed with him the covenant He had made with Abraham and Isaac.

B. Jacob and Laban *(Genesis 29:1–31:55)*

Arriving at his destination, Jacob soon discovered the home of his uncle, Laban. There he fell in love with Rachel, Laban's younger daughter. Laban required him to work seven years in order to receive this daughter in marriage. Jacob carried out his part of the bargain, only to be deceived by Laban, who at the wedding substituted Leah, his older daughter. Laban later gave Rachel to Jacob in marriage, but he was forced to work an additional seven years for her.

After this Jacob remained with his father-in-law for six more years, making a total of twenty years spent there. God blessed Jacob during this period, giving him eleven sons and a daughter by his two wives and their handmaidens. God also caused his flocks to increase greatly. But tensions mounted between Jacob and Laban, and so Jacob decided to return to the land of his youth, taking with him his wives, his children, and his flocks. Upset by Jacob's sudden departure, Laban pursued him as far as the hill country of Gilead. But after a confrontation, the two men settled their differences and went their separate ways.

C. Back Home *(Genesis 32:1–33:17)*

As Jacob approached the land of his youth, he had another problem. Esau still lived there, and Jacob feared he might yet bear a grudge for the treatment he had received at Jacob's hands. Jacob tried to prepare the way by sending gifts to Esau. But before the two brothers met, Jacob was confronted by an extraordinary man. Hosea 12:4 calls him an angel; Jacob himself called him God (32:30). Jacob wrestled with this being through the night, and from him received a blessing and a new name— Israel, meaning "he struggles with God."

When the two brothers finally met, Jacob was surprised to find that Esau bore him no ill will. Esau had his faults, but he had grown rich and powerful. Under those circumstances he was quite willing to let bygones be bygones. After this, Jacob settled in Canaan, living first at Shechem, then at Bethel, and later at Hebron.

IV. Joseph

The closing chapters of Genesis tell the familiar story of Joseph. Because of his faithfulness to God, Joseph is one of the most attractive persons in the Old Testament. As a child, he received special favors from his father because his mother was Jacob's favorite wife. Joseph's brothers came to hate him because of this, and Joseph, who as a lad became a bit spoiled by his father's attention, contributed further to their dislike by his actions.

A. From Slave to Ruler *(Genesis 37:1-36; 39:1–41:57)*

It is not surprising, then, that when Joseph came to visit his brothers they plotted to kill him. However, Reuben was able to talk them out of that bloody deed. They sold Joseph to some Ishmaelite and Midianite merchants, who took him to Egypt. There he was sold as a slave to Potiphar, one of Pharaoh's officials.

Because of his ability and his integrity, Joseph soon rose to a position of trust in Potiphar's house; but when he rejected the advances of Potiphar's wife, he was thrown into prison. Through the power of God he was able to interpret the dreams of Pharaoh's cupbearer and baker, who had been put in jail because they had displeased the Pharaoh. Eventually Joseph was called from the prison to interpret the Pharaoh's dreams. Joseph informed the king that his dreams indicated there would be seven good years followed by seven years of famine. Pharaoh was so impressed that he made Joseph his second-in-command. Joseph's task was to collect the extra grain grown in the good years and store it in preparation for the lean years that were to follow.

B. The Family Reunited *(Genesis 42:1–50:26)*

When the famine years came, they affected not only Egypt but Palestine as well. Before long, Joseph's brothers and his father Jacob were feeling the results. Hearing that grain was available in

Egypt, Jacob sent the ten brothers there to purchase some. Only Benjamin, the youngest, remained at home with his father. When they arrived in Egypt, Joseph immediately recognized them. Though he bore them no ill will, he set about testing them.

When Joseph finally revealed himself to them, they were fearful lest he seek revenge for the wrongs they had done him. But Joseph's only emotion was joy at the reunion. He recognized that his brothers' sinful act had been used of God to fulfill His purposes. "It was not you who sent me here," he said, "but God" (Genesis 45:8). When the Pharaoh learned of this happy reunion, he insisted that Jacob and all his family be invited to move to Egypt, where they were settled in the rich land of Goshen in the Nile delta.

Jacob and his family—his wives, children, and grandchildren—numbered sixty-six. These, along with Joseph, his wife, and two sons, totaled seventy. The descendants of Jacob, the children of Israel, would eventually number in the hundreds of thousands before they finally escaped from Egypt some four hundred years later. The closing chapters of Genesis tell of the death of Jacob and Joseph. We are also told of Joseph's reassuring words that God would lead them out of Egypt and into the land of promise (Genesis 50:24).

The Exodus and Conquest

Exodus 1:1—Joshua 24:33

The previous chapter closed with the people of Israel living in Goshen in Egypt. There they prospered and multiplied. But after some centuries a Pharaoh came to the throne "who did not know about Joseph." Some historians believe that the Pharaoh was Thutmose III or Thothmes III, a powerful king of the eighteenth dynasty.

I. Birth and Education of Moses *(Exodus 1:8–2:25)*

This Pharaoh became apprehensive about the Israelites, not only because they had become so numerous, but also because Goshen was on the route that enemies might take should they invade Egypt. To have so many foreigners living there might be an invitation for enemies to attack. The Pharaoh's plan was to reduce the Israelites to slavery. This, he supposed, would stop them from increasing in number, and their forced labor would also allow him to enhance his reputation as a builder of great cities. But the plan didn't work. In spite of restrictions the Israelites continued to become more numerous.

Finally, in an act born of frustration and anger, the Pharaoh ordered that all sons born to Hebrew parents must be cast into the river. We can only guess how many parents went through the agonizing experience of obeying this decree. But at least one set of parents, Amram and Jochebed, chose to disobey when Moses was born to them. After hiding the baby for three months, they realized that they would soon be detected if they continued to keep him. And so they placed him in a basket made of papyrus reeds coated with tar and pitch so that it would float. They placed the basket in some reeds along the Nile.

No doubt they hoped against hope that somehow he would escape the death that seemed certain. Their hope was realized when Moses was found by the Pharaoh's daughter, who took him to rear as her own son. We can see God's hand working through all this to prepare a man who would one day lead His people to freedom. Because he was reared in Pharaoh's court, Moses was educated in the wisdom of ancient Egypt and he also knew Egyptian ways.

But Moses' own mother shared in his rearing, and he was never allowed to forget that he was a Hebrew. Later when he saw an Egyptian mistreating a Hebrew, his loyalty to his own people welled up in him and he killed the Egyptian. As a result of this rash act, committed when he was about forty, Moses had to flee Egypt. He found refuge in Midian in the desert near Mount Sinai. There Moses married Zipporah, the daughter of a priest named Jethro or Reuel, and settled down to tending his father-in-law's flock. He spent about forty years in this activity before God was ready to use him. This period of learning patience and self-control was apparently necessary for Moses, but it was also necessary that the Israelites be persecuted to the point where they would be willing to listen to God's leader when he came.

II. The Exodus *(Exodus 3:1–15:21)*

God's call to Moses came in a most dramatic way—God spoke to him in a bush that burned but was not consumed (Exodus 3:2). When Moses turned aside to see this startling phenomenon, God spoke to him. Moses was challenged to return to Egypt and lead the people out of that country. Moses immediately began to make excuses, but one by one God answered these until he had no choice but to go. It is not surprising that the Pharaoh rejected Moses' call to let the children of Israel go, and as a result God sent ten terrible plagues upon the land.

The tenth and last plague, which brought death to the firstborn of every household in Egypt, was the most devastating of all. The only households spared in this tragedy were those of the Israelites

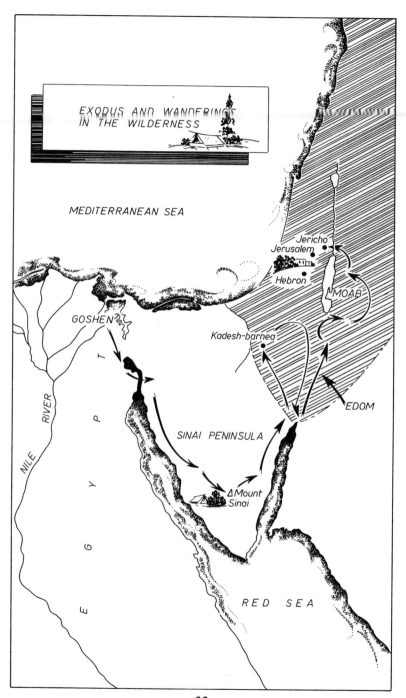

EXODUS AND WANDERINGS IN THE WILDERNESS

MEDITERRANEAN SEA

GOSHEN

Jericho
Jerusalem
Hebron

MOAB

Kadesh-barnea

EDOM

E G Y P T

NILE RIVER

SINAI PENINSULA

△ Mount Sinai

RED SEA

who had observed the feast of the Passover. Each family took a lamb, killed it, dressed it, and roasted it. They took some of the blood from the lamb and sprinkled it on the tops and sides of the doorframes. Then when the Lord came in the night, He passed over the houses so marked, sparing the firstborn in those households. As a part of this observance, the Israelites were to eat bread that had been prepared without yeast. This is the origin of the feast of the Passover, which Jews observe even to this day.

When death struck the firstborn of the Pharaoh, that proud monarch relented and gave permission for the children of Israel to leave Egypt. When God led them out of Egypt, He did not take them by the direct route that ran along the seacoast. Rather, He led them by the desert road by the Red Sea. To show the way, He went before them in a pillar of cloud that became fire at night.

The Israelites had barely gotten on the road when Pharaoh again changed his mind and decided to pursue them and force them to return. The result was one of the greatest miracles recorded in the Old Testament, one that the Israelites referred to again and again in their later history.

Pharaoh was certain that he had the Israelites trapped against the sea, but then God moved the pillar of cloud to stand between the Egyptian army and the Israelites. God then ordered Moses to stretch out his staff over the sea, and when he did, the sea opened up, allowing the people to cross over on dry land. But when the Pharaoh's army attempted to follow, the sea closed upon them, destroying them.

III. The Wilderness *(Exodus 15:22–Deuteronomy 34:12)*

The Israelites were now free of Egypt and needed no longer to fear the Pharaoh. But they were quickly confronted by other problems. For one thing, there was little water in the desert; but Moses led them to springs or God miraculously provided water. Their food supplies were soon exhausted, but God gave them a bread-like material, which they called manna, and quail for meat. Yet no matter how adequately God provided for them, they continued to grumble.

In the third month they arrived at the foot of Mount Sinai. Moses then ascended the mountain, where God gave him the Ten Commandments, engraved on two tablets of stone. (See Exodus 20:1-17.) Moses was on the mountain for forty days. During his absence the people grew restless and persuaded Aaron to make a golden calf for them. After offering sacrifices before it, they engaged in a wild orgy of eating and reveling. When Moses returned to the camp, he was furious at what he found, and in his anger he broke the tablets. Then he ground up the golden calf, sprinkled the dust on water, and forced the people to drink the water.

Later Moses returned to the mountain, where once more the Ten Commandments were inscribed on tablets. In addition God gave Moses elaborate instructions for building the tabernacle, a tent in which worship would be conducted. God also gave Moses detailed instructions for preparing sacrifices and for the priests who would conduct the worship. Workers were chosen to begin to build the tabernacle. When it was completed, God's glory in the form of a pillar of cloud by day and a pillar of fire by night came to rest upon it.

The book of Leviticus gives detailed instructions for carrying out worship in the tabernacle. The three great feasts were Passover, Pentecost, and Tabernacles. Also important was the annual Day of Atonement. In addition, there were other feasts, including the feast of Trumpets and the feasts of the sabbatical year and the year of jubilee.

The book of Numbers begins by telling of a census of the people, which was taken by tribes, clans, and families. The census showed that there were about six hundred thousand men of Israel capable of bearing arms, in addition to the women and children. On the basis of this number it has been estimated that there were two and a half million or perhaps three millions persons in the Israelite camp.

Numbers 13 tells that twelve spies were sent into the promised land. When they returned, they had some good news and some bad news. The good news was that the land was fruitful, flowing with milk and honey. But the bad news was that it was inhabited by people who were numerous and powerful and who lived in fortified cities. Ten of the spies were fainthearted and reported that the Israelites could never stand against such a powerful enemy. But the other two spies, Caleb and Joshua, urged the people to go forward and possess the land.

Frightened by the unfavorable report, the people began to complain. Finally they threatened to kill Moses, Aaron, Joshua, and Caleb. As the people prepared to take violent action, the glory of the Lord appeared in the tabernacle. God was prepared to send a plague upon them and blot them out and then raise up a new nation from Moses. But Moses, who loved his people in spite of their rebellious ways, lifted up a prayer to God on their behalf (Numbers 14:13-20).

God heard Moses' prayer and spared the people, but at the same time He decreed that all persons over twenty except Joshua and Caleb would perish in the desert. Instead of moving directly into the promised land, the Israelites would spend the next thirty-eight years wandering around in the wilderness because of their rebellion.

Numbers 16 tells of a rebellion led by Korah, who desired to oust Moses and Aaron and seize power. As punishment, the earth opened up and swallowed him and his comrades. Another 250 who joined with them were consumed by fire. But still the people were rebellious the next day, and so 14,700 were struck down by the plague. Following this, God vindicated Moses and Aaron in a dramatic way by causing Aaron's rod to blossom.

After these tragic events, the people continued their long sojourn in the desert, which lasted forty years from the time they left Egypt. Before long, Miriam, the sister of Moses, died. Then at Meribah, Moses was guilty of the sin that was to keep him out of the promised land. The people were grumbling because they had no water. God told Moses to speak to a rock so that it would send forth water. But instead, Moses, perhaps because of his irritation with the people, struck it with his staff. Water came forth as God had promised, but because Moses and Aaron had rebelled (Numbers 20:24) they were denied the privilege of leading the people into Canaan. Some time after this incident, Aaron died on top of Mount Hor. His son, Eleazar, took his place as high priest.

During this period of wandering, the people continued to murmur and complain. This time God sent poisonous snakes among them to punish them. Many died as a result, and so the people were brought to repentance. Moses was instructed to make a bronze snake and place it upon a pole. Those who had been bitten by a snake could look upon the bronze snake and be spared. Jesus later mentioned this as a symbol of His death on the cross. In a similar fashion, those who turn to Him will not perish (John 3:14, 15).

As they continued their wandering, various nations tried to stop them but were unsuccessful (Numbers 21). Sihon, king of the Amorites, and Og, king of Bashan, were disastrously defeated by

36

the Israelites. As a result of these victories, the Moabites were filled with fear. Their king, Balak, sought to thwart the invaders without facing them in battle. He sent messengers to bring the prophet Balaam to pronounce a curse upon the Israelites, but Balaam had his problems (Numbers 22). As he rode to confer with Balak, the angel of the Lord, invisible to Balaam but seen by his donkey, stood in his path, threatening with a drawn sword. One can't help chuckling a bit at the scene that followed as Balaam learned a valuable lesson from his donkey. Later when Baalam tried to bring a curse upon Israel, God sent blessings instead.

The opening chapter of the book of Deuteronomy finds the Israelites in the desert country east of the Jordan River in the fortieth year of their wanderings. Much of the book is given to preparing the people for their entrance into the promised land. Moses knew that his time was short and that Joshua would soon become the leader. Moses tried to warn the people against the dangers of idolatry (Deuteronomy 4) and in chapter 5 he reminded them of the Ten Commandments and the conditions under which God had given them.

In Deuteronomy 6:4, 5 we find the "shemah," the very heart of the Hebrew faith: "Hear, O Israel: The Lord our God, the Lord is one. Love the Lord your God with all your heart and with all your soul and with all your strength." These words are followed by the admonition to the fathers to teach God's words to their children at every possible opportunity. We today may well consider this admonition. Each generation has the duty of teaching God's Word to the generation that follows.

The closing chapter of Deuteronomy tells of the Israelites' renewing of their covenant with God. Moses reminded the people of the mighty works God had performed in their behalf and assured them of His continued blessing if they would remain faithful. His challenge to them was brief and to the point: "I set before you today life and prosperity, death and destruction" (Deuteronomy 30:15). Clearly, these two options left no room for compromise.

With this final challenge to the people, Moses' great work was completed. Leaving the people, who were then camped in Moab east of the Jordan River, Moses made his way to the top of Pisgah. There God allowed him a glimpse of the promised land that stretched out before him from Dan in the north to the Negev in the south, from the valley of the Jordan to the western sea (the Mediterranean). Having been granted this panoramic view of the land, Moses died and was buried in a grave known only to God. Perhaps God kept the place secret to prevent the tomb from becoming a shrine, which it certainly would have become had men known its location.

IV. The Conquest

At Moses' death the leadership of the children of Israel fell to Joshua, one of the two faithful spies. His immediate task was to move the people across the Jordan and against the Canaanite tribes that then occupied the land. First of all, however, spies were sent out to observe the territory into which they were to advance. Two spies entered the fortified city of Jericho, but their mission was soon discovered. They were able to escape only because of the ruse of Rahab, the prostitute, who hid them and helped them escape over the city wall. In turn, they gave her assurance that she and her household would be spared when the city fell to the Israelites. Interestingly, Rahab is named in the ancestry of Jesus (Matthew 1:5).

When the time came for the people to cross the river, the priests carried the ark of the covenant ahead of them. As soon as their feet touched the water, it miraculously receded. The people were able to cross over on dry land (Joshua 3). Their first objective was Jericho, which God through a mighty miracle delivered into their hands. But because Achan hid some of the spoil from Jericho for his own use, the Hebrew force was humiliated at Ai. Only after Achan was discovered and punished did God allow them to capture that town (Joshua 7, 8).

Hearing the fate of Jericho and Ai, the people of Gibeon by deception gained a treaty with Joshua that spared their city. Then when a coalition of Amorite kings sought revenge against the Gibeonites, Joshua came to their rescue. In the battle that followed, God caused the sun to stand still so that the Hebrews' victory could be complete (Joshua 10:1-15).

Following this, Joshua turned his forces to the south. One by one he defeated the Canaanite towns from Kadesh Barnea to Gaza (Joshua 10:29-43). Next he moved to the north and attacked the cities there, winning victory after victory. Soon the whole land was, for all practical purposes, under the control of the children of Israel (Joshua 11).

We may find the brutal destruction of the Canaanite towns and population a shocking thing. We need to keep in mind that the wickedness of the Canaanites had reached such depth that God's judgment was poured out upon them. Archaeologists have uncovered evidence that they practiced human sacrifice, engaged in unspeakable sexual orgies, and participated in vile idolatry. For hundreds of years God had tolerated these things in order to give the people an opportunity to repent. Now, with Joshua as His instrument of judgment, God was meting out justice.

Following the conquest of the land, it was divided among the tribes (Joshua 13—19). Each tribe except the Levites received a portion. The Levites, from whom came the priests and who served about the tabernacle, were given certain towns, and they were to receive their support from the other tribes (Joshua 21).

The book of Joshua closes with that intrepid leader's ringing challenge: "Choose for yourselves this day whom you will serve, whether the gods your forefathers served beyond the River, or the gods of the Amorites. . . . But as for me and my household, we will serve the Lord" (Joshua 24:15).

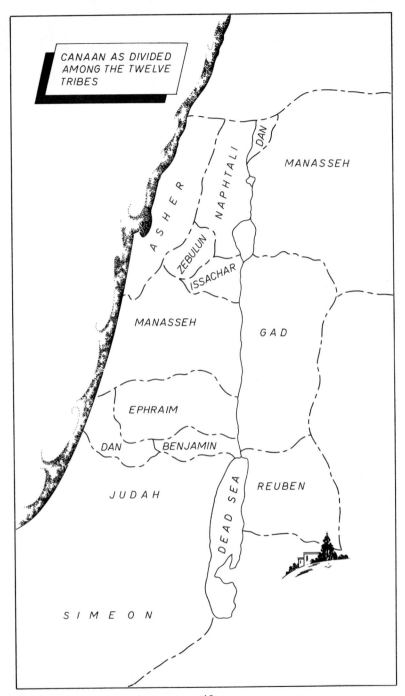

CANAAN AS DIVIDED AMONG THE TWELVE TRIBES

ASHER

NAPHTALI

DAN

MANASSEH

ZEBULUN

ISSACHAR

MANASSEH

GAD

EPHRAIM

DAN

BENJAMIN

JUDAH

DEAD SEA

REUBEN

SIMEON

The Period of the Judges

Judges 1:1—1 Samuel 10:25

I. The Difficult Times of the Judges

A. The Historical Cycle *(Judges 2:6-19)*

The period that extended from the death of Joshua to the time
of Saul, covering about three hundred years, was a difficult one
for the children of Israel. Neither God's wonderful blessings during the Exodus and conquest nor the suffering that came upon
them when they sinned had worked to bring them to spiritual
maturity. Once in the promised land they should have been prepared to prosper in a land flowing with milk and honey. But all
too readily they were seduced by the pagan religions of their
neighbors or fell victim to their own lusts and divisive spirit.

Lacking the leadership that had earlier been provided by Moses
and Joshua, the people fell into a state that was usually disorga-
nized and often even approached anarchy. Such a condition left
them open to attack by their neighbors, who rarely missed an
opportunity to persecute them.

The book of Judges, since it reports only a few of the incidents
of the period, is not intended to be a complete history of those
times. Rather, it is written for the purpose of moral and religious
instruction. As we study the book, a series of cycles is revealed to
us. At the start of the cycle the people are enjoying prosperity.
Then they fall into sin. As a result of their sin, God permits them

41

to be oppressed, and they suffer greatly. This suffering then leads to repentance. Finally, when they repent, God restores their prosperity, and the cycle is completed. Before long, however, they once more fall into sin and the whole agonizing cycle is repeated. Let us watch for this cycle—sin, suffering, repentance, restoration—throughout the book.

B. The Work of the Judges *(Judges 3–16)*

After Joshua died there were still many people living who remembered their life in the wilderness and the stirring days in which they had conquered the promised land. Knowing what great things God had done for them, they were faithful to Him. But those people finally passed from the scene, and "another generation grew up, who knew neither the Lord nor what he had done for Israel. Then the Israelites did evil in the eyes of the Lord and served the Baals" (Judges 2:10, 11). As a result, God did not drive out all of the Canaanitish tribes, but allowed some of them to remain to become a test for the Israelites. When the Israelites grew evil and idolatrous, God would allow a heathen tribe to conquer them and oppress them by taking a large part of their livestock and harvest, or demanding tribute of silver or gold. Then when the people would straighten up their lives and worship God, He would raise up a judge to lead them in defeating the oppressors. We know very little about most of these judges, but what little we do know shows us that they do not fit neatly into a mold. They are quite varied in their backgrounds, their conduct, and their moral commitments. About the only thing they share in common is a willingness to be used of God to relieve Israel's oppression.

1. Othniel *(Judges 3:7-11)*

The first of these judges specifically named is Othniel, a nephew of Caleb. He was able to overpower Cushan-Rishathaim, king of Aram Naharaim in Mesopotamia, giving the land peace for forty years.

2. Ehud and Shamgar *(Judges 3:12-31)*

Once more the Israelites fell into sin, and God allowed the Moabites to oppress them. Ehud, who was left-handed, concealed a sword on his right thigh when he went to carry tribute to Eglon, king of Moab. When the opportunity arose, he drew the sword, assassinated the king, and made his escape. Later he returned with an Israelite army and defeated the Moabites, giving the land peace for eighty years.

Ehud was followed by Shamgar, who struck down six hundred Philistines with an oxgoad, giving Israel another respite from persecution.

3. Deborah *(Judges 4, 5)*

Not all the judges were men. One of the most capable and respected of them was a woman, Deborah. She is called a "prophetess" (Judges 4:4), and for several years she held court under a palm tree between Ramah and Bethel. There she dispensed justice to all who came to her with disputes. Since there were no laws requiring this, it would seem that she had gained the respect and support of the people through her prophetic insights and the impartial justice she meted out.

During this time Israel fell under the power of Jabin, the king of Canaan, whose headquarters were in Hazor. Deborah summoned Barak and gave him the Lord's command to defeat Jabin's general, Sisera. But Barak was willing to go only if Deborah would go with him. Deborah did accompany him, but she assured him that because of his fear of going alone, he would receive none of the credit.

With Deborah giving the orders, Barak plunged into battle and defeated the Canaanites in spite of their superiority in chariots. Sisera, fleeing the battle afoot, took refuge in the tent of Jael. As soon as he fell asleep, she drove a tent peg through his temple and later delivered his dead body to Barak. It was indeed a day of victory for Israel—and for the woman who had engineered it. Judges 5 is Deborah's victory song.

4. Gideon *(Judges 6:1–8:35)*

But Deborah's victory was not permanent. The terribly monotonous refrain was repeated again! "The Israelites did evil in the eyes of the Lord, and for seven years he gave them into the hands of the Midianites" (Judges 6:1). The Midianites ravaged the land, driving the Israelites to despair. Then in their desperation they cried out to the Lord.

God answered their cries by sending the angel of the Lord to call Gideon into His service. Gideon was reluctant at first to take such a responsibility, but the angel finally convinced him to

43

accept the call. One of the first things Gideon did was to tear down his father's altar to Baal and cut down a symbol or pole dedicated to Asherah. After this episode and after receiving a sign from God in the wet and dry fleece, Gideon was ready to take on the Midianites.

Gideon was able to recruit an army of thirty-two thousand; but to his dismay, the Lord told him that this was too large for the task at hand. Through God's direction, he reduced his forces to three hundred men. Then, using a subterfuge, he surprised the Midianites so completely that they fell upon one another and fled in panic. The Gideons International, an organization that distributes Bibles in hotels, hospitals, and colleges, takes its name from this Old Testament character. The symbol of this organization is a jar or pitcher, reminiscent of the jars used by Gideon.

5. Abimelech, Tola, and Jair *(Judges 9:1–10:5)*

Following Gideon's victory the land enjoyed peace for forty years: but just as soon as Gideon died, the people turned once again to their idols. Abimelech, Gideon's son by a concubine, took this opportunity to seize control by murdering seventy of his half-brothers. Only the youngest son, Jotham, escaped this carnage.

Citizens of Shechem supported Abimelech in this coup, but soon they turned against him. In the civil war that followed, Shechem was destroyed. But those who live by violence often perish by violence. Abimelech met his end when a woman dropped a millstone on his head when he was attacking another city.

Abimelech was followed by Tola and Jair. They are given only brief mention, and so we know little of what happened during the period of their judgeships (Judges 10:1-5). But once these two had passed from the scene, the Israelites began again the same old cycle, doing evil in the sight of God and serving the Baals and the Ashtoreths. This time Israel was overcome both by Philistines from the west and by Ammonites from the east.

6. Jephthah *(Judges 10:6–12:7)*

Then out of the depths the people once more cried out to God, who heard their pleas and called Jephthah to liberate them from the Ammonites. Jephthah defeated the Ammonites, but before going into battle he had made a vow that he would sacrifice as a

44

burnt offering whatever came out of his house to meet him when he returned from battle. The joy of his victory turned to sorrow when his only daughter came out to greet him. Some scholars believe that, instead of being offered as a burnt offering, she was dedicated to the service of the Lord and not permitted to marry, remaining a virgin the rest of her life (Judges 11:34-39). Whether that was the case or not, Jephthah's tragedy serves as a warning to any who are tempted to make rash vows.

A bloody civil war between the Ephraimites and the Gileadites led by Jephthah followed this episode. During the war the famous password, *Shibboleth,* was used by the men of Gilead to identify the Ephraimites (Judges 12:5, 6).

7. Ibzan, Elon, and Abdon *(Judges 12:8–13:1)*

Three obscure judges—Ibzan, Elon, and Abdon—followed Jephthah. After Abdon died, the people of Israel soon fell into sin again. This time they were punished by a forty-year oppression at the hands of the Philistines. These pagans from the Mediterranean coast proved to be a source of suffering for Israel until well into the reign of David.

8. Samson *(Judges 13:2–16:31)*

The stories of Samson's life and his marvelous feats of strength have been frequently told in Sunday-school lessons in which he has been depicted as a great hero for Israel. A hero he was, but unfortunately he was a hero with feet of clay. His birth was foretold by the angel of the Lord. The boy was to be a Nazirite of God: that is, one specially dedicated to God, who drank no alcoholic beverages and ate nothing unclean during his entire life. For the defense of his people God gave him matchless strength and magnificent courage. He could tear a lion apart with his bare hands (Judges 14:5, 6). With only a bone for a weapon, he could attack an army and slaughter a thousand men (Judges 15:14-16).

Samson's first big mistake was falling in love with a Philistine woman. Nothing would do but that his parents would arrange for his marriage to her. This led to all kinds of complications, including lasting antagonism between Samson and the Philistines (Judges 14:1—15:16).

Samson's problems with foreign women continued. On another occasion, he went down to Gaza where he visited a prostitute. The Philistines sought to kill him, but he escaped by carrying off the city gates (Judges 16:1-3).

Samson's downfall came at the hands of another woman, Delilah, presumably also a Philistine. She used her charms to deliver him into the hands of his enemies. Samson's death was both tragic and heroic. His weakness for women left him blinded and at the mercy of the Philistines, but in his final act he destroyed the temple of Dagon along with many of the Philistine leaders. Perhaps the great lesson of Samson's life is that God can use a person whose personal life is seriously flawed.

The closing chapters of Judges paint a dismal picture of conditions in Israel. Many fell into idolatry, violence was commonplace, and strife between the tribes led to a civil war that almost exterminated the tribe of Benjamin. The closing verse of the book (Judges 21:25) tells us why virtual anarchy existed: "In those days Israel had no king: everyone did as he saw fit." This sounds very much like our own times when every person wants to do his own thing.

C. The Book of Ruth *(Ruth 1–4)*

Yet in the midst of this dark scene there glitters a precious jewel—the book of Ruth. Here we see that not all the people of Israel were deep in idolatry and immorality. The leading characters, and indeed all the people of Bethlehem, appear as gentle, generous, upright, and God-fearing people. This little book tells the true story of a Moabite woman who remained loyal to her mother-in-law, Naomi, in face of many difficulties, including the death of her husband, her father-in-law, and her brother-in-law. In the end her loyalty was rewarded as she became the wife of Boaz. To them was born a son, Obed, who became the grandfather of King David. Thus Ruth, a Moabitess, has a place in the lineage of Christ (Matthew 1:5).

II. A Time of Change *(1 Samuel 1–10)*

The opening chapters of 1 Samuel tell of the birth of that great leader who gives his name to the book. He served in the period of transition between the judges and the kings of Israel.

A. Samuel's Birth *(1 Samuel 1:1–2:11)*

The marriage of Hannah and Elkanah was not blessed with children. This became a heavy burden for Hannah, for in ancient

Israel a childless wife was held up for ridicule and pity. On one of her visits to the tabernacle, which was then located at Shiloh, Hannah prayed fervently that God would give her a son. So intense was her supplication that Eli, the high priest, thought she was intoxicated and started to reprimand her for coming drunk to the place of worship. When she told Eli of her wish, he pronounced this blessing upon her, for she had promised that if she should bear a son, she would dedicate him to the Lord.

God answered her prayer, and a son was born to her about 1080 B.C. She called him Samuel, which means "asked of God." Much as she treasured her baby, she did not forget her vow to dedicate him to the Lord. When he was weaned, she took him to the tabernacle and left him in the care of Eli, the priest. Each year she made him a robe and took it to him when she and Elkanah visited the tabernacle. Samuel continued to grow both in stature and in favor with God and man (1 Samuel 2:18-21, 26).

B. Eli's Wicked Sons (1 Samuel 2:12–4:22)

Eli, a good man, was plagued by two wicked sons, Hophni and Phinehas, who desecrated the house of worship with their wickedness. Eli was told of their activities and he rebuked them, but he did not take any decisive action to stop their abuses. As a result, a man of God, an unnamed prophet, warned Eli that both his sons would die on the same day.

The prophecy was fulfilled when the two sons accompanied the ark of the covenant into battle against the Philistines. Not only were Hophni and Phinehas killed, but the ark was captured by the Philistines and carried to Ashdod. When this tragic news was brought to Eli, the old man fell off his chair and broke his neck.

C. Samuel Becomes the Leader (1 Samuel 5:1–10:25)

Disaster followed the Philistines who had captured the ark, and so they returned it. For twenty years it remained at Kiriath Jearim. During this time the people repented at Samuel's preaching. They recognized that God was using him to lead them.

When the Israelites were in a meeting at Mizpah, the Philistines came up to attack them. But the Lord was with Samuel, and the people repulsed the attack and defeated the invaders. To commemorate this victory, Samuel raised a memorial stone, which he called Ebenezer, meaning "Stone of help," for he said, "Thus far had the Lord helped us" (1 Samuel 7:12).

Samuel continued as a judge over the people for many years, going on a circuit from Bethel to Gilgal to Mizpah. When he grew older, Samuel appointed his two sons, Joel and Abijah, as judges to assist him. Unfortunately, his sons were like the sons of Eli. They brought disrepute upon their office by taking bribes and perverting justice. Dismayed by such abuses, the people asked for a king. Samuel was displeased, feeling that the people were rejecting him. But God consoled him by assuring him that the one being rejected was not Samuel, but God himself.

Samuel tried to talk the people out of their wish for a king. He pointed out the demands a king would make on them. But the people refused to listen. They wanted to be like the nations about them, and those nations all had kings. Resigning himself to the people's determination, Samuel awaited God's guidance in the matter. Finally God pointed out His choice, Saul. Samuel then anointed Saul (1 Samuel 10:1) as king and later introduced him to the people (1 Samuel 10:23, 24). The people were impressed when they saw him, for he stood a head taller than anyone else. Gladly they hailed him: "Long live the king!"

Judges and Early Kings of Israel

Judges About 1370-1050 B.C.

Oppressor	Years of Oppression	Judge	Years of Leadership
Aram (Syria)	8	Othniel	40
Moab	18	Ehud	80
Philistines		Shamgar	
Canaan	20	Deborah/Barak	40
Midian	7	Gideon	40
		Abimelech	3
		Tola	23
		Jair	22
Philistines/Ammonites	18	Jephthah	6
		Ibzan	7
		Elon	8
Philistines	40	Samson	20
		Samuel	

Early Kings About 1050-931 B.C.

Saul	40
David	40
Solomon	40

Division of the Kingdom About 931 B.C.

Saul and David

1 Samuel 10—1 Kings 2

The period of about eighty years from 1050 to 970 B.C. was a glorious one for the kingdom of Israel. From the anarchy, both moral and political, that prevailed during the period of the judges, the kingdom emerged first as a place of growing political stability and then as a place of growing prosperity. By the end of David's reign, Israel was rapidly becoming the dominant power on the land bridge that connected Mesopotamia to Egypt. It is not surprising, then, that generations that followed looked back on this period and idealized it.

I. The Reign of Saul (1 Samuel 10—31)

A. Early Victories (*1 Samuel 11:1-11; 13:1–15:9*)

The shouts at Saul's coronation had scarcely died away when he was faced with a crisis. The Ammonites had besieged the town of Jabesh Gilead, demanding that the inhabitants submit to humiliating slavery. Men of that town appealed to Saul, who was then at Gibeah, for help. Saul immediately sent a challenge to all of Israel to support him in a rescue mission. With the support mustered by this appeal, Saul was quickly able to field an army that routed the Ammonites.

Saul's next foe was the Philistines. They proved to be a most formidable enemy, for they had iron weapons, while the Israelites were not yet so armed. Nevertheless the Israelites succeeded in routing the superior forces of the Philistines, largely through the bravado of Saul's son, Jonathan. This venture almost ended in tragedy when Saul sought to carry out a rash vow he had made before the battle. Only the intervention of the troops prevented Saul from taking his own son's life.

Saul waged other successful military campaigns, not only against the Philistines but also against other surrounding tribes. Notable among these victorious campaigns was that against the Amalekites, whom God told Saul to exterminate completely.

B. Disobedience (1 Samuel 13:5-14; 14:47, 48; 15:10-35)

In preparing for the conflict with the Philistines, Saul made his first big mistake. His troops were assembled at Gilgal. They were to await the arrival of Samuel, who was to preside over the burnt offering. When Samuel was delayed, Saul became impatient and offered the sacrifices on his own. This incident gives a valuable clue to Saul's impetuous personality. It also led to Samuel's pronouncement that Saul's kingdom would not endure.

Saul was disobedient again when God sent him to utterly destroy the Amalekites along with all their animals. Saul's attack succeeded, but he kept back some of the animals for a sacrifice, and made the king a prisoner. Samuel rebuked him sternly. Saul protested that he had obeyed God's order, but Samuel would have none of his lame excuse. "To obey is better than sacrifice," he thundered, "and to heed is better than the fat of rams!" Then Samuel repeated his earlier proclamation that God had rejected Saul as king because of Saul's disobedience. After this Samuel and Saul went their separate ways—Samuel to Ramah and Saul to Gibeah—never to meet again.

C. David's Appearance on the Scene (1 Samuel 16, 17)

Before long, Samuel was sent to the household of Jesse to anoint a new king. God there led Samuel to anoint David, Jesse's youngest son. Saul began to experience periods of deep depression, which apparently could be soothed by the music of a harp. Young David was called into Saul's service as a musician. It seems that this was only part-time service, however. David went back home when Saul did not need him.

Saul soon found himself in another conflict with the Philistines. It was on this occasion that David appeared on the scene to champion the Israelite cause against the giant, Goliath. After that, David no longer went back home. He became an officer in Saul's army (1 Samuel 18:1-5).

D. Saul's Hatred of David *(1 Samuel 18–30)*

Jonathan and David became devoted friends, but Saul's friendship for David soon ended. Saul's jealousy was aroused when he and his troops came home in triumph. As the people came out to meet the army, they sang of Saul's victory over thousands, but David's victory over tens of thousands. Saul could not bear to hear such acclaim for anyone but himself. He began to plot ways to get rid of David. But God was with David, and one plot after another was foiled. Saul gave David his daughter, Michal, in marriage; but even that was part of a plot to get rid of him (1 Samuel 18:20-27).

Saul's hatred of David grew more intense as his plots failed, and finally David was forced to flee. Both Jonathan and Michal dared their father's wrath to defend David and help him escape. Much of the remainder of Saul's reign was spent in pursuit of David. On more than one occasion David had a chance to kill Saul, but each time he refused to harm the king. His loyalty to Saul in spite of mistreatment is notable, and so is his respect for God's anointed king. Such virtues our age might well imitate.

E. Saul's Death *(1 Samuel 31)*

Saul's tragic end came in a battle against the Philistines on the slopes of Mount Gilboa. Prior to the battle, Saul had gone to consult with a medium or witch at Endor. In the seance Samuel appeared, not to comfort Saul, but to remind him of the judgment he had brought upon himself (1 Samuel 28:4-25).

In the battle that followed, Saul's three sons were killed and Saul himself was wounded. Faced with torture and death at the hands of the Philistines, Saul fell on his sword, taking his own life. Thus concluded a reign that started with great potential but ended in disaster because of disobedience.

II. The Reign of David *(2 Samuel 1–1 Kings 2)*

Many years before Saul's death, Samuel had announced that because of Saul's disobedience he had forfeited his throne. As a result, Samuel had anointed David in anticipation of Saul's death. Now David was prepared to step onto the stage as king.

A. David Becomes King *(2 Samuel 1:1–5:3)*

When David heard of Saul's death, he sincerely lamented the tragedy in a noble elegy (2 Samuel 1:19-27). David still maintained a profound respect for the royal office in spite of Saul's abuse of it. When an Amalekite came claiming that he had killed Saul, apparently hoping for a reward, David ordered him executed on the spot for killing the Lord's anointed.

At first David's following was largely in Judah, and so he made Hebron his capital. In the meantime, Abner, the commander of Saul's army, had installed Saul's son, Ish-Bosheth, on the throne with the support of the Benjamites and the northern tribes. A bitter civil war followed, in which Joab, David's commander, bested Abner. When Abner saw that the situation was running against him, he abandoned Ish-Bosheth and attempted to make a deal with David. When Joab learned of this, he treacherously murdered the wily old commander. Soon after, Ish-Bosheth was also murdered, leaving no serious claimant to the throne except David. Though David benefited from these murders, he had nothing to do with them and renounced them publicly. His conduct won the respect of the other tribes, and leading men came to Hebron to make David king of all Israel.

B. David's Move to Jerusalem *(2 Samuel 5–7)*

After reigning in Hebron seven and a half years, David captured the Jebusite fortress at Jerusalem and took up residence there. It was a wise move. Jerusalem was strategically located, and its site could be readily fortified and protected.

David was determined to make Jerusalem a religious center as well as a political capital. To do this, he arranged to have the ark of the covenant placed in a tabernacle in Jerusalem (2 Samuel 6). However, he was not content to see the ark remain in a tent while he himself lived in a palace. He wanted to build a temple, but God forbade that because David was a man of war (1 Chronicles 28:3). The building of the temple was reserved for his son, Solomon.

C. David's Conquests *(2 Samuel 8–10)*

After David had consolidated his control over all the tribes, he turned his attention to the enemies who had become a threat to the people during the closing years of Saul's reign. First he defeated the Philistines, whom he reduced to subserviency. Never again were these dreaded enemies to pose a serious threat to

Israel. The Moabites also were defeated, and the survivors compelled to pay tribute. With the decline of the Assyrians and the Hittites, a power vacuum developed into which the Syrians rapidly expanded. Their actions seemed to threaten Israel, and so David went to war against them and defeated them.

In similar fashion, the Edomites to the south and the Ammonites with their Aramean mercenaries were defeated. Though surrounded by powerful enemies on every side, David by courage and able strategy was able to bring victory to his nation. (Modern Israel, surrounded as she is by Arab enemies, must feel a sense of kinship with ancient Israel in this respect.)

Just as David could be valiant in battle, so he could be magnanimous in victory. His attitude toward Ish-Bosehth was one example of this (2 Samuel 4:5-12). His treatment of Jonathan's son, Mephibosheth, was another. Mephibosheth had been crippled while a child, and both his feet were lame. Yet as a descendant of Saul, he might have been able to gather a following and threaten David's claim to the throne. It was the usual practice in the Orient when a man gained the throne for him to put to death all of the former king's heirs, thus protecting himself against a future revolt. Yet David refused to do this in the case of Mephibosheth. Instead, he took him into his own house and provided for him the rest of his life (2 Samuel 9).

D. David's Later Tragedies *(2 Samuel 11–22)*

David's great victories and the growing affluence these victories brought caused this noble king to lower his spiritual guard, and he eventually fell victim to terrible sins. He was attracted by Bathsheba and committed adultery with her. To cover his sin, he conspired to have her husband, Uriah, killed in battle. Seemingly the plot went undetected, but even as David began to congratulate himself upon committing a perfect crime, God's spokesman, Nathan, confronted him. Murder, even when committed by a king, will out. Nathan's parable about a poor man's lamb taken by a rich man aroused David's ire without arousing his suspicions. Then as David's anger reached the boiling point, Nathan pointed the accusing finger at him: "You are the man."

Nathan took a calculated risk in making the accusation, for David might very well have disposed of Nathan as he had Uriah. But instead, David humbly confessed his guilt and accepted the judgment that the prophet pronounced upon him. The child born to David and Bathsheba died. David went through a period of almost uncontrolled mourning. Out of his experience David wrote two very moving psalms: Psalm 51 in which David confessed his guilt, and Psalm 32 in which he expressed the relief that came from the forgiveness of sin.

Though David experienced forgiveness for his sins, yet his actions sowed seeds that were to bear bitter fruit. His son Amnon fell in love with his half-sister, Tamar, and eventually became so impassioned that he raped her. This enraged her brother Absalom, who sought revenge. He waited patiently for two years, and then made an opportunity to kill Amnon. All of this must have brought considerable grief to David, but eventually he forgave Absalom and was reconciled to him.

Absalom, who was a striking young man, soon had a following among the people. This undoubtedly fed his ambition, and he secretly began to plot against his father. When he felt the time was ripe, he issued a call for insurrection to begin. The revolt came as a surprise to David, and he was forced to flee Jerusalem. But in the ensuing conflict, Absalom was killed and David was restored to his throne.

E. David's Last Years (2 Samuel 24–1 Kings 2)

Though the final years of David's reign were generally peaceful, yet some tragic events marred them. One of these incidents was David's effort to conduct a census of the fighting men. As a result, a pestilence fell upon the land.

Another major crisis developed near the end of David's life when one of his sons, Adonijah, attempted to seize the throne. Nathan and Bathsheba were in the meantime working to insure that Solomon would succeed his father. Such a power struggle often developed between half-brothers in the polygamous households of Oriental kings. In this struggle, Adonijah's efforts failed and Solomon became the next king when David died.

Such a complex man as David defies easy analysis. He was, first of all, a man of his own times. This explains some of his bloodthirsty activities, even if it does not excuse all of them. He was a man of deep compassion, as evidenced at the death of his son Absalom. He on occasion fell into terrible sin; yet he had a deep sense of guilt over his sins and knew true repentance. For all his weaknesses he stands as one of the greatest men of the Old Testament, a man truly after God's own heart (1 Samuel 13:14).

The Reigns of Solomon and Rehoboam to the Division of the Kingdom

1 Kings 2—12

The reign of Solomon is sometimes called the golden age of Israel, and that designation is appropriate in many ways. David had succeeded in crushing most of Israel's enemies, so there were no serious threats from the minor powers about. Further, the greater powers of Egypt and Mesopotamia were in a period of decline, freeing Solomon from fears of invasion. During his reign there was a vast increase in foreign trade and in building programs, including the temple, that dotted the land with impressive structures.

I. Solomon Gains the Throne *(1 Kings 1–4)*

A polygamous household is usually filled with plots and intrigues. The household of David was no exception. As the aging king neared his death, Adonijah sought to seize the throne.

A. The Plot of Adonijah *(1 Kings 1, 2)*

Adonijah had several things going for him. He was handsome, and he was older than Solomon. Thus he came to believe that he should succeed his father, and so he began to line up his support—Joab, the old warrior, and Abiathar, the priest. Seeing that David was increasingly feeble, and perhaps on his deathbed, Adonijah felt that the time had come to make his move. He invited all his brothers (except Solomon) and many of the leaders of Israel to a gathering near En Rogel, a spring located outside the southeast corner of Jerusalem. There he sacrificed a great number of sheep and cattle, giving a feast in an endeavor to gain support for his claims.

When word reached Bathsheba, she acted quickly to secure the throne for her son. Calling Nathan the prophet, Zadok the priest, and Benaiah the captain of David's guard to her aid, she persuaded David to appoint Solomon king. David granted her wishes and Solomon was anointed.

Learning of this turn of events, Adonijah's guests quickly departed. Fearing for his life, Adonijah himself fled to the altar for sanctuary. Solomon graciously granted him amnesty, provided he would conduct himself properly. But Adonijah made the mistake of asking for Abishag, David's nurse during his final illness. In the Oriental world this was readily interpreted as an attempt to claim the throne. Solomon ordered Adonijah executed for his presumptuous act. Abiathar the priest was removed from office and exiled to his home in Anathoth for his part in the plot. Joab, who had been guilty of the blood of others, suffered the same violent fate he had meted out in the past. He too sought sanctuary at the altar, but Solomon ordered him executed anyway. With his enemies dead or exiled, Solomon was free to claim the throne without any serious challenge.

B. Solomon's Request for Wisdom *(1 Kings 3, 4)*

At the beginning of his reign, Solomon went to Gibeon to worship. There God appeared to him in a dream, saying, "Ask for whatever you want me to give you" (1 Kings 3:5). Solomon humbly recognized his own lack of experience, and then asked God to give him a discerning heart that he might rule his people wisely.

Solomon's response pleased the Lord, especially because he asked for wisdom rather than for long life or wealth. As a result, God granted him the wisdom he requested, but in addition He promised him wealth and honor.

II. Solomon's Building Activities

Almost as soon as he ascended the throne, Solomon embarked upon a series of ambitious building programs that were to change the face of Palestine.

A. The Building of the Temple *(1 Kings 5, 6)*

The temple is, of course, the most famous of these projects. David had hoped to build the temple and provide a permanent place for the ark of the covenant, but God had forbidden this. David had, however, done some of the preliminary planning and had made arrangements for many of the materials for the temple (1 Chronicles 22:1-5; 28:11-19).

Solomon employed the services of Hiram of Tyre to supply timber for the building, both pine and the famous cedar of Lebanon. Thirty thousand men were employed in the lumbering efforts. Another eighty thousand were used as stonecutters, with an additional seventy thousand working as carriers, not counting thirty-three hundred who were foremen.

The site selected for the temple was the eastern of the two main hills upon which Jerusalem is built. This was the threshing floor of Araunah purchased by David. It is generally believed that this was the spot where Abraham was prepared to offer up Isaac. Today a Moslem structure, the Dome of the Rock, is there.

The foundations of the temple were laid in the fourth year of Solomon's reign, and it took more than seven years to complete the temple itself, making its completion date about 960 B.C. The stone for the building was cut and shaped at the quarry so that "no hammer, chisel or any other iron tool was heard at the temple site while it was being built" (1 Kings 6:7).

The temple was ornately decorated, and its furnishings were fabulous. Gold was lavishly used, and "nothing was made of silver, because silver was considered of little value in Solomon's days" (1 Kings 10:21). Since the price of gold fluctuates so widely, it would be impossible to estimate the value of the gold used in the temple, but certainly its worth today would run into millions of dollars.

B. Other Building Activities

Solomon also built a palace for himself that took thirteen years to build and dwarfed the temple in size if not in splendor. He also built the throne hall where he conducted the business of his kingdom (1 Kings 7:1-12). Many of the stones used in the foundations were massive. It is believed that some of these stones can still be seen in the walls of Jerusalem.

In addition to these buildings, Solomon constructed chariot cities for his horses and chariots. These were strategically placed about his kingdom to provide for its defense. He built also store cities and other cities throughout his kingdom (1 Kings 9:15-19).

III. Solomon's Diplomatic and Trade Activities

David spent much of his time fighting to build and maintain his kingdom. Solomon, on the other hand, resorted to diplomacy to accomplish his ends.

A. Solomon's Foreign Wives

Israel's rise to power brought with it temptations to compromise her religious convictions. Egypt could have been a threat to Solomon and his ambitions. To prevent this, a marriage was arranged between Solomon and the Pharaoh's daughter (1 Kings 3:1). While this assured him of cordial relations with Egypt, it brought into Israel corrupting religious influences. Many other political marriages were arranged, involving women from many of the surrounding nations—Moabites, Ammonites, Edomites, Sidonians, and Hittites (1 Kings 11:1).

God had told the Israelites that they were not to intermarry with such foreigners, lest the women turn them to strange gods. And that is exactly what happened to Solomon: "As Solomon grew old, his wives turned his heart after other gods, and his heart was not fully devoted to the Lord his God" (1 Kings 11:4). On the hill to the east of Jerusalem, Solomon built "high places," places of worship, for the gods Chemosh and Molech. There his foreign wives burned incense and offered sacrifices to them.

The example Solomon set for his people in this matter certainly created many problems. The fact that he had seven hundred wives and three hundred concubines made a normal home life impossible. In this respect, too, the king failed to set a good example for his people.

B. Solomon's Treaties

Solomon used diplomacy to maintain friendly relations with many of his neighbors. Most notable among these was Hiram, king of Tyre. Not only did Hiram provide workers and materials for the temple; he also operated an extensive merchant fleet for Solomon (1 Kings 9:26-28; 10:11, 22).

These political arrangements allowed Solomon to enter many profitable trade agreements with the surrounding nations. Solomon and Israel grew rich as a result of this extensive trade. Yet

59

the tragedy was that so much of this wealth was wasted on frivolous things and vain displays. The common people probably enjoyed little direct benefit from all this vast increase in wealth.

IV. Solomon's Famous Wisdom

Perhaps Solomon was most famous for his wisdom. Very early in his reign he gained a well-earned reputation for his sagacity. He had prayed to God for wisdom to rule his people well, and God had answered his prayer bountifully. He was knowledgeable in matters of science, especially about living things. His wisdom extended to literary accomplishments, including three thousand proverbs and more than a thousand songs (1 Kings 4:29-34). Most of the book of Proverbs, the Song of Solomon, and Ecclesiastes are attributed to him.

A. Common Sense

Solomon also had practical common sense. When two women quarreled about who was the real mother of a baby, he proposed to cut the baby in two, giving each mother half. Faced by this threat, the real mother, in order to spare the child's life, relinquished her claim. Thus Solomon was able to establish the fact that she was the real mother (1 Kings 3:16-28).

B. The Visit of the Queen of Sheba *(1 Kings 10:1-13)*

Word of Solomon's wisdom spread widely, eventually reaching the land of Sheba, located in southwestern Arabia or perhaps in Ethiopia. Desiring to behold him with her own eyes, the queen of that land made the long trip to Jerusalem. Seeking to probe the breadth and depth of his wisdom, she tested him with hard questions and riddles. But he passed the examination with flying colors: "nothing was too hard for the king to explain to her" (1 Kings 10:3).

She was also impressed by his palace, his wealth, the food on his table, the servants that surrounded him, and even the offerings he made in the temple. Her summary, spoken with amazement, was "not even half was told me" (1 Kings 10:7).

V. An Evaluation of Solomon's Reign

Solomon's reign began most promisingly with his humble and sincere prayer for God's guidance. But God's blessings had in them the seed of Solomon's destruction. As his wealth increased, so did his taste for a lavish life-style. His building programs, which certainly contributed to his sense of pride, exacted a heavy price from the people, who were sometimes reduced to virtual slavery to meet his demands.

Even more serious problems arose because of his polygamous marriages. The Scriptures tell us that he had seven hundred wives and three hundred concubines (1 Kings 11:3). Many of these were foreign wives who brought with them their pagan religions. The presence of pagan religions soon led many of the Israelites astray.

In the book of Ecclesiastes, Solomon reveals himself as a tired old man, jaded by his life of indulgence. He had tried work, wealth, pleasure, and many other activities, but none brought lasting pleasure, only vanity. The closing words of the book give sound advice, advice that he had not always applied in his own life: "Remember your Creator in the days of your youth, before the days of trouble come. . . . Fear God and keep His commandments, for this is the whole duty of man, for God will bring every deed into judgment" (Ecclesiastes 12:1, 13, 14).

God did bring judgment upon him. Because he had been disobedient, God would, during the reign of Solomon's son, divide the kingdom, leaving only a fragment (1 Kings 11:9-13).

VI. Rehoboam Ascends the Throne *(1 Kings 12)*

A. Foolish Actions *(1 Kings 12:1-15)*

Following the death of Solomon, Rehoboam went to Shechem for his coronation. There representatives of the people asked him to reduce the heavy tax burden Solomon had imposed upon them. Rehoboam's wise old counselors advised him to listen to the people and grant them some tax relief.

But Rehoboam was not pleased with this advice and turned to his young counselors. They urged him to ignore the people's just demands and heap even greater burdens upon them. Rehoboam foolishly followed their advice.

B. The Kingdom Divided *(1 Kings 12:16-24)*

The people turned to Jeroboam for leadership. Jeroboam had agitated against Solomon during the latter days of his reign. As a result, he had fled to Egypt for refuge, but upon learning of Solomon's death, he returned, ready to lead the revolt against Rehoboam. In the confrontation that followed, Adoniram, Rehoboam's forced-labor superintendent, was stoned to death. The king himself barely escaped with his life. Rehoboam was left with only the one southern tribe of Judah. The little tribe of Benjamin soon returned to him, however, giving his kingdom two tribes (1 Kings 12:20, 21). This division of the kingdom is usually dated 931 B.C.

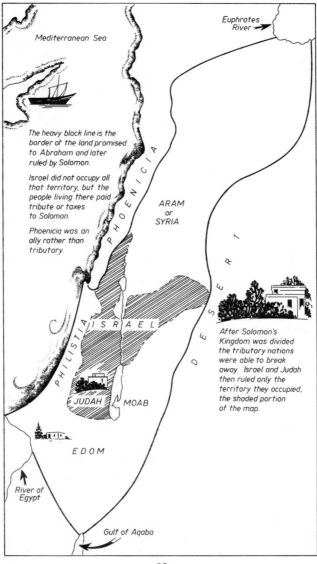

Mediterranean Sea

Euphrates River →

The heavy black line is the border of the land promised to Abraham and later ruled by Solomon.

Israel did not occupy all that territory, but the people living there paid tribute or taxes to Solomon.

Phoenicia was an ally rather than tributary.

PHOENICIA

ARAM or SYRIA

DESERT

PHILISTIA

ISRAEL

JUDAH

MOAB

After Solomon's Kingdom was divided the tributary nations were able to break away. Israel and Judah then ruled only the territory they occupied, the shaded portion of the map.

EDOM

River of Egypt

Gulf of Aqaba

Apostasy in the Northern Kingdom (931-722 B.C.)

1 Kings 11—2 Kings 17

In the two centuries that followed the division of the kingdom, the northern part, often referred to as Israel and sometimes as Ephraim, moved steadily toward her ultimate destruction. There were times of revival and a return of political and military power, but as a whole the picture is one of steady decline until the final destruction of Samaria by the Assyrians in 722 B.C. It is sobering to realize that the United States has not lasted quite this long, yet we can see within it some of the same weaknesses that finally sapped the strength of Israel.

I. The Dynasty of Jeroboam (931-910)

Jeroboam had risen to prominence during Solomon's reign. One day he was approached by the prophet Ahijah, who proceeded to tear his new cloak into twelve pieces. Ten of these, representing the northern tribes, he gave to Jeroboam, informing him that some day he would be ruler over these tribes. Perhaps this spurred Jeroboam into rebellious acts, for soon Solomon sought his life and he had to flee to Egypt (1 Kings 11:26-40).

A. Jeroboam's Religious Apostasy

Once Jeroboam ascended the throne, he began to consolidate his power. He selected Shechem as his capital and fortified it.

63

Realizing that he would have trouble retaining the loyalty of the people as long as they continued to visit Jerusalem regularly to worship in the temple, he set up two golden calves, one at Bethel and one at Dan. Since both of these towns had been considered sacred places, they naturally attracted the people (1 Kings 12:25-30).

Probably Jeroboam intended the golden calves to represent symbolically the presence of God, yet in the minds of the people they quickly became objects of worship. He also initiated other changes in the accepted religious practices. Among other things, he selected priests who were not from the tribe of Levi; he set up altars in high places; and he established new feast days (1 Kings 12:31-33).

On one occasion as Jeroboam stood at the altar to make a sacrifice to God, a prophet reproached him. When Jeroboam sought to order the man arrested, the king's hand was miraculously shriveled. At his pleading, the prophet then prayed that God would restore it. But even this experience did not convince Jeroboam that he should change his ways (1 Kings 13:1-6, 33, 34).

During much of his reign, Jeroboam carried on a series of border wars with Judah (1 Kings 14:30). Neither side could totally defeat the other, but both Israel and Judah were weakened. God withdrew His protection because idolatry and other sins were rampant in Judah as well as Israel. Therefore Pharaoh Shishak of Egypt was able to invade both countries in 926 B.C. and defeat them. His conquest of Judah is recorded in 1 Kings 14:25-28. Shishak's own record, carved on a temple wall at Karnak, indicates that he overran Israel also.

B. Succeeded by Nadab (910)

Following Jeroboam's reign, his son, Nadab, came to the throne (1 Kings 14:20). But he reigned only two years before he was murdered by Baasha (1 Kings 15:25-28).

II. The Dynasty of Baasha *(909-886 B.C.)*

Once he had gained the throne, Baasha proceeded to murder all the members of Jeroboam's family (1 Kings 15:29). Jeroboam had lived in Tirzah during part of his reign, and now Baasha took up his residence there. He ruled for twenty-four years (1 Kings 15:33), but he did not restore righteousness in the land. Like Jeroboam, "he did evil in the eyes of the Lord."

64

Relations were never good between Baasha and Asa, the king of Judah at this time. The two leaders were often at war (1 Kings 15:32). Baasha "did evil in the eyes of the Lord," continuing to walk in the sins of Jeroboam (1 Kings 15:34).

When Baasha died, his son Elah came to the throne. After only two years, he was the victim of a plot by Zimri, who caught him drunk at a party and murdered him. Proclaiming himself king, Zimri then murdered all of the family of Baasha. But Zimri's reign lasted only seven days before he was opposed by Omri, commander of the army. When Omri besieged his royal palace at Tirzah, Zimri set fire to the palace and perished in the flames (1 Kings 16:8-19).

III. The Dynasty of Omri (885-841 B.C.)
1 Kings 16–22; 2 Kings 1–9
A. Omri's Rule (885-874 B.C.)

Following Zimri's death, Israel was divided. Some chose to follow Omri, and others preferred Tibni. After five years the followers of Omri prevailed, and Omri became king. He reigned six years in Tirzah, and then he moved the capital to Samaria, where it was to remain until the fall of Israel (1 Kings 16:21-24).

Omri proved to be a capable ruler who brought stability to the northern kingdom. Some scholars think he established friendly relations with Ethbaal, king of Tyre and Sidon, by arranging the marriage between his son, Ahab, and Ethbaal's daughter, Jezebel. This marriage was to prove disastrous for Israel, because Jezebel brought her pagan deities and priests along with her to Israel (1 Kings 16:30-33).

B. Ahab's Rule (874-853 B.C.)

At Omri's death in 874 B.C., Ahab came to the throne. He was a capable ruler who was able to maintain Israel's military strength that his father had built up. But he also resorted to diplomacy to accomplish his ends. He established friendly relations with Jehoshaphat, king of Judah, cementing this agreement by the marriage of his daughter, Athaliah, to Jehoshaphat's son, Jehoram (2 Chronicles 18:1; 21:5, 6). Ahab's own marriage to Jezebel, a Phoenician princess, insured good relations with Tyre and Sidon.

Israel's archenemy was Syria or Aram, with its capital at Damascus. Ahab defeated the Syrian king, Benhaded, causing him to come begging for his life. Ahab spared the notorious Benhadad, not necessarily because he was merciful, but because he felt the Syrian would be more useful to him as a live ally than as a dead enemy. However, by sparing the life of Israel's dreaded enemy, Ahab incurred the condemnation of the prophet of God (1 Kings 20:26-43).

Ahab also carried out extensive building activities. In addition to enhancing Samaria, he built for himself in Jezreel a lavish house of stone and wood, decorated with inlaid ivory. Archaeological evidence indicates that many other cities were built or enlarged by Ahab (1 Kings 21:1; 22:39).

C. The Ministry of Eiljah

Ahab's weakness was shown when he allowed Jezebel to import into Israel her Baal worship, along with scores of priests of Baal and Asherah. As a result, Baal worship was not limited to Jezebel. Soon many Israelites were enticed by the sexual orgies involved in the worship of these pagan deities. But Jezebel was not content with this. She persuaded Ahab to embark on a program of persecution designed to destroy the prophets of Jehovah (1 Kings 18:4).

In these difficult times the prophet Elijah was called to proclaim the word of God. In his austere life-style and his uncompromising stand, he stood in stark contrast to Ahab. Elijah appeared suddenly on the scene to confront Ahab for his iniquity. Elijah pronounced the judgment of God on the wicked king: Israel would suffer a prolonged drought (1 Kings 17:1). Having delivered his message, the prophet took refuge in Kerith, where he was sustained with water from a brook and food brought by ravens (1 Kings 17:2-6).

Then just as suddenly, after the drought had weakened Ahab, Elijah appeared once more and challenged Ahab to bring his false prophets to Mount Carmel for a showdown. In dramatic fashion the power of Jehovah over Baal was demonstrated. The people, who had at first refused to take a stand with Elijah, then turned and attacked the false prophets, killing all of them (1 Kings 18:1-40).

But Elijah, so courageous when facing the prophets of Baal, turned tail and ran when Jezebel vowed to kill him. Fleeing to the desert country south of Beersheba, he felt so discouraged and alone that he prayed that God would allow him to die. But God strengthened him, reminding him that there were yet seven thousand in Israel who had not bowed down to Baal. Then God sent him on a mission to anoint Hazael king over Syria and Jehu over Israel, and also to enlist his own successor, Elisha (1 Kings 19:1-21).

Elijah had yet another confrontation with Ahab. This one came when Jezebel plotted to have Naboth killed so that Ahab could have his vineyard. When Ahab went down to take possession over the vineyard, there the rugged prophet stood to pronounce doom upon him: "Where dogs licked up Naboth's blood, dogs will lick up your blood!" (1 Kings 21:19).

D. Ahab's Death *(1 Kings 22:1-40)*

In Assyria, far to the northeast, the powerful Shalmaneser III had come to the throne. Seeking to enlarge his empire, he launched a campaign against the Syrians. In the Battle of Karkar he inflicted heavy losses on the forces of Benhadad and Ahab. Soon those two allies had a falling out. For this conflict, Ahab gained the support of Jehoshaphat of Judah. Before going into battle, Ahab was warned by the faithful prophet Micaiah that his venture would prove fatal. But Ahab ignored the warning and suffered a mortal wound by an arrow launched by chance. The dire prophecy of Elijah was fulfilled (1 Kings 22:37-38) as dogs licked up the blood of the king.

E. The End of a Dynasty

Ahab was succeeded by his son, Ahaziah, who almost immediately faced rebellion in Moab. But before he could take strong action, he was injured in a fall. Then because he sought help from Baal rather than Jehovah, he died (1 Kings 22:40; 2 Kings 1:1-18).

Since Ahaziah had no son, his brother Joram or Jehoram succeeded him. At about this same time, Elijah was taken up into heaven in a whirlwind, having passed his mantle or cloak to Elisha as a sign that Elisha was his successor (2 Kings 2:1-14).

In several well-known incidents Elisha gave evidence that the power of God rested upon him. He miraculously provided oil for a widow and restored a Shunammite's son to life (2 Kings 4:1-37). Other miracles included the healing of Naaman, a leper, and the thwarting of a Syrian army sent to capture Elisha (2 Kings 5:1-19; 6:8-23).

IV. The Dynasty of Jehu *(2 Kings 9, 10, 13, 14)*

A. Jehu's Reign (841-814 B.C.)

Elisha arranged to have Jehu anointed king even before Joram died (2 Kings 9:1-10). The messenger declared that it was God's will that the house of Ahab be completely destroyed. With these words ringing in his ears, Jehu went forth to seize the throne. He killed both Joram and Ahaziah, the king of Judah. Then he went to Jezreel and had Jezebel killed. He followed this with a bloody purge of Ahab's descendants and their friends and advisors (2 Kings 9:11—10:17).

Jehu followed this by destroying the ministers of Baal and their temple. By this ruthless purge, he sought to root out every vestige of Baalism. Yet he continued in the sins of Jeroboam by allowing the golden calves to stand at Dan and Bethel (2 Kings 10:18-29).

The violence of Jehu in killing Jezebel alienated Tyre and Sidon, and his killing of Ahaziah alienated Judah. And so when Hazael, King of Syria, began to press upon Israel, Jehu had nowhere to turn for help. As a result, he was unable to prevent the Syrian king from annexing some of his territory (2 Kings 10:32).

From the northeast the Assyrian power was once more turning its attention to Syria and Palestine. The powerful Shalmaneser invaded these two countries and exacted tribute from them. On the famous black obelisk of Shalmaneser, now in the British Museum, one may see the figure of Jehu bowing down before Shalmaneser.

B. Jehoahaz and Jehoash (814-782 B.C.)

Jehoahaz, who succeeded his father Jehu, inherited a kingdom that had been weakened by wars and invasions. Things were a bit better under his son Jehoash, because Assyria suppressed Syria and gave Israel a bit of breathing room and time to recover some of the territory she had lost earlier. In fact, Jehoash captured Amaziah, the king of Judah, and attacked Jerusalem, carrying away some of the treasures from the temple and the king's palace (2 Kings 13:1-25; 2 Chronicles 25:21-24).

C. The Prosperous Reign of Jeroboam II

The most powerful ruler of the dynasty of Jehu was Jeroboam II, who ruled from 782-753 B.C. He was able to recover the territory that Israel had previously lost, taking even Hamath and

68

Damascus in the north and Moab and Ammon east of the Jordan. He refortified Samaria and made it a rich and luxurious city. Archaeologists have discovered about two hundred ivory plaques, probably used as inlays on furniture or on the walls of houses (2 Kings 14:23-29).

Yet these military successes and material achievements could not obscure the wickedness and oppression that were prevalent in the land. The prophet Amos, who lived during the latter days of Jeroboam's reign, aimed his verbal barbs at some of these iniquities: Woe to "you women who oppress the poor and crush the needy" (Amos 4:1); "the houses adorned with ivory will be destroyed" (Amos 3:15); "woe to you who . . . lie on beds inlaid with ivory" (Amos 6:1, 4).

The prophet Hosea also lived during this period. The burden of his ministry was that Israel had abandoned Jehovah, her first love, to play the harlot in pursuit of false gods.

Jeroboam's son Zechariah was the last member of this dynasty. After reigning only six months, he was assassinated by Shallum. The heritage of violence that Jehu had stored up now paid full dividends as his dynasty ended in violence (2 Kings 15:8-12).

V. The Last Kings of Israel *(2 Kings 15, 17)*

The end for the northern kingdom, Israel, was not far away. Shallum, who came to the throne by murdering Zechariah, ruled only a month before he himself became the victim of a similar plot by Menahem (2 Kings 15:13, 14). Menahem's reign lasted ten years (752-742 B.C.) We are told that he did evil in the eyes of the Lord and "did not turn away from the sins of Jeroboam" (2 Kings 15:16-18).

During Menahem's reign, Pul (also known as Tiglathpileser), the king of Assyria, invaded Syria and Palestine. To persuade him to leave, Menahem had to pay him a sizeable tribute (2 Kings 15:19, 20). In one of his inscriptions, Tiglathpileser mentions receiving tribute from "Menahem of Samaria."

Menahem's son, Pekahiah, followed him to the throne. Pekahiah reigned only two years before he was assassinated by one of his officers, Pekah (2 Kings 15:22-25).

Pekah joined Rezin of Damascus in an alliance against Assyria. They sought to force Ahaz, king of Judah, into the alliance, but he refused and appealed to Assyria for help. Tiglathpileser once more turned his attention westward, crushing the Syrians and

69

killing Rezin, attacking Israel, and reducing Judah to a vassal state (2 Kings 15:27-30; 16:5-9).

After an eight-year reign, Pekah was assassinated by Hoshea. Under Hoshea, Israel remained a vassal of Assyria, paying heavy tribute at regular intervals. Finally, however, Hoshea grew tired of this heavy burden. Hoping to receive help from Egypt, he revolted against the Assyrian king, Shalmaneser V. The results were easily predictable. The Assyrians besieged Samaria, which after three years fell to the invaders, now led by Sargon II. Some twenty-seven thousand prisoners were taken to Assyria and scattered about the empire. Captives were brought in from other places and settled in Israel, leading to a racial mixture that emerged as the Samaritans later in history.

God's inspired writer informs us why this suffering was visited upon Israel. "All this took place because the Israelites had sinned against the Lord their God" (2 Kings 17:1-7).

The Divided Kingdom—Israel and Judah

Division of the Kingdom   About 931 B.C.

Kings of Judah	Kings of Israel	Prophets
Rehoboam 931-913	Jeroboam 931-910	
Abijam 913-911	Nadab 910-909	
Asa 911-870	Baasha 909-886	
	Elah 886-885	
	Zimri 885	
	Tibni 885-880	
Jehoshaphat 870-848	Omri 885-874	
	Ahab 874-853	Elijah
	Ahaziah 853-852	
Jehoram 848-841	Jehoram 852-841	Elisha
Ahaziah 841		
Athaliah 841-835	Jehu 841-814	
Joash 835-796	Jehoahaz 814-798	Joel
Amaziah 796-767	Jehoash 798-782	Jonah
Azariah 767-740	Jeroboam II 782-753	Amos
(Uzziah)	Zechariah 753-752	Hosea
		Isaiah
	Shallum 752	Micah
	Menahem 752-742	
	Pekahiah 742-740	
Jotham 740-736	Pekah 740-732	
Ahaz 736-716	Hoshea 732-722	

End of Northern Kingdom of Israel About 722 B.C.

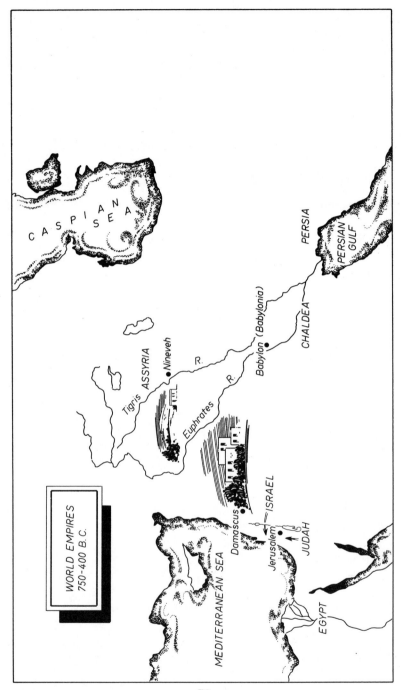

WORLD EMPIRES
750-400 B.C.

CASPIAN SEA

PERSIA

PERSIAN GULF

CHALDEA

Babylon (Babylonia)

Tigris R.

ASSYRIA

Nineveh

Euphrates R.

ISRAEL

Damascus

Jerusalem

JUDAH

MEDITERRANEAN SEA

EGYPT

Ups and Downs of the Southern Kingdom 931-716 B.C.

1 Kings 12—2 Kings 16; 2 Chronicles 10—28

Introduction

The division of Israel left the southern kingdom, Judah, weak and isolated. Yet her very isolation may have been a blessing in disguise, for she did not become enmeshed in the worship of pagan gods so quickly as did Israel. Further, her geographical isolation meant that she did not so frequently suffer the incursion of invading armies.

Judah had her share of troubles, for like Israel she had some wicked kings. Yet she also had some good kings whose reforming efforts served to purge the land of pagan idolatry. But in the end even these reformers were not enough to keep Judah from going the way of Israel.

I. The Early Kings

A. Rehoboam *(1 Kings 12:1-24; 14:21-31)*

In a previous chapter we have discussed Rehoboam's accession to the throne following the death of his father, Solomon. His rash action in refusing to consider the complaints of the northern tribes led to the division of the kingdom in 931 B.C. It almost led to his own death at the hand of the angry northerners.

Yet Rehoboam was not totally to blame for the rebellion. Solomon, by laying heavy burdens on the people in his extravagant building programs, had made many subjects very unhappy. We need also to recognize that the tribes had never been firmly bound together. A good deal of dissension, even civil war, had gone on among them. Since settling in the promised land the people had been united only during the reigns of Saul, David, and Solomon. Even David faced problems early in his reign, and only after several years was he able to establish control over the entire nation.

When the northern tribes revolted, Rehoboam mobilized an army to reestablish his control over them. But the prophet Shemaiah brought the word of God forbidding any such campaign (1 Kings 12:21-24). Rehoboam obeyed the Lord at that time, yet the Scriptures say, "There was continual warfare between Rehoboam and Jeroboam" (1 Kings 14:30). There must have been numerous border clashes between the forces of the two nations.

In spite of the loss of the northern tribes, Rehoboam seems to have prospered. One reason for this was that many of the priests and Levites, offended by the idolatrous worship instituted by Jeroboam, migrated to Jerusalem. So did many others who were seeking the Lord (2 Chronicles 11:13-17). Yet religious conditions in Jerusalem were little better than those in the north. The pagan shrines built for many of Solomon's foreign wives were allowed to remain. Enticed by these, many people "set up for themselves high places, sacred stones, and Asherah poles on every high hill and under every spreading tree." They also began to engage in many other detestable practices of their heathen neighbors, including male prostitution (1 Kings 14:23, 24).

Rehoboam had other problems. The alliance his father had forged with Egypt was falling apart. The pharaoh, Shishak, had harbored Jeroboam when he had fled from Solomon (1 Kings 11:40). About 927 B.C., after the kingdom had divided, Shishak invaded Judah and attacked Jerusalem, carrying off many treasures from the temple (1 Kings 14:25).

B. Abijah *(1 Kings 15:1-8; 2 Chronicles 13:1-22)*
After reigning seventeen years, "Rehoboam rested with his fathers," and his son Abijah reigned in his stead. Abijah's rule lasted only two or three years, during which time he continued the border wars with Israel that his father had started. Also "he committed all the sins his father had done before him; his heart was not fully devoted to the Lord his God" (1 Kings 15:3).

C. Asa (911-870 B.C.)
1 Kings 15:9-24; 2 Chronicles 14–16).

Abijah was succeeded by his son Asa, whose long reign of forty-one years brought peace and prosperity to Judah. Soon after the beginning of his reign, he began a religious reform that rid the land of the idols and male prostitutes. He even deposed his grandmother because she had made an Asherah pole.

When Zerah the Cushite, who ruled Egypt, marched against Judah with a large army, Asa, with the help of God, defeated him and drove him and his army from the land. Egypt then did not pose a serious threat to Judah for many years.

Near the end of his reign, however, Asa had problems with Baasha, king of Israel, who fortified the city of Ramah, just north of the border of Judah. Asa saw in this a threat, and so he mobilized his own forces in defense. But he did not trust his own defenses, and so he sent many of the treasures from the temple to Benhadad of Syria to bribe him to attack Israel on the north. The scheme worked, and Asa was able to capture Ramah and carry away the materials that had been accumulated to build its defenses. But this action was condemned by Hanani the seer because Asa had trusted in the king of Aram (also called Syria) rather than in God. Rather than repent, Asa became angry at the prophet and had him thrown into prison (2 Chronicles 16:7-10).

II. Jehoshaphat to Amaziah
A. Jehoshaphat (870-848 B.C.)
2 Chronicles 17:1–21:1

Jehoshaphat must certainly rank among the greatest of the kings of Judah. He was dedicated to restoring the true worship of Jehovah to his kingdom, and so he continued many of the reform efforts begun by his father. He was also interested in religious education. He sent officials with Levites to instruct the people in the book of the law of the Lord (2 Chronicles 17:7-9).

He also made provisions for a more adequate administration of justice throughout his realm. He established courts in the fortified cities of Judah and set up a system of appellate courts (2 Chronicles 19:4-11). He charged his judges to judge carefully because "you are not judging for man but for the Lord" (2 Chronicles 19:6).

Jehoshaphat strengthened the defenses of Judah by fortifying many towns and by keeping a large standing army. These measures, along with his godliness, won him respect abroad (2 Chronicles 17:10-19). From his position of strength Jehoshaphat was able to enter into a treaty with Israel that prevented the recurring wars between the two states that had marred earlier reigns (2 Chronicles 18:1). This alliance produced more harm than good, however. Jehoshaphat shared Israel's defeat by Syria (2 Chronicles 18). Later he lost heavily in a joint merchant marine (2 Chronicles 20:35-37). Worst of all, Jehoshaphat's son Jehoram was married to Athaliah, pagan daughter of Ahab and Jezebel. This woman brought tragedy to Judah after Jehoshaphat's reign was over.

B. Jehoram (848-841 B.C.)
2 Kings 8:16-24; 2 Chronicles 21

The religious reforms that Jehoshaphat brought to Judah proved to be only temporary, for Jehoram soon began to undermine them and introduce Baalism. Apparently Athaliah, like her mother Jezebel, was an ardent missionary for the religion of Baal; and like her mother she was strong enough to dominate her husband.

Jehoram began his reign by putting all of his brothers to the sword. His religious apostasy so weakened the land that Edom soon revolted against him. In trying to put down the revolt, his army was shattered and he was almost captured. The Philistines and Arabs also attacked Judah and carried off the king's wives and sons.

He ended as miserably as he had ruled, his death resulting from a terrible and painful disease of the bowels. The chronicler related that "he passed away, to no one's regret," and was not even buried in the tombs of the kings (2 Chronicles 21:20).

C. Ahaziah (841 B.C.)
2 Kings 8:25-29; 9:27-29; 2 Chronicles 22:1-9

Ahaziah followed his father to the throne. His older brothers had all been killed by raiding Arabs. He reigned only a year, and probably it was just as well, because "he walked in the ways of the house of Ahab, for his mother encouraged him in doing wrong" (2 Chronicles 22:3). His mother was Jezebel's daughter, Athaliah, still bent on doing evil!

Ahaziah met his death in Israel. He went to visit the king of Israel, who had been wounded in battle. Both kings were killed in

Jehu's purge when he seized the throne for himself (2 Chronicles 22:7-9).

D. Athaliah (841-835 B.C.)
2 Kings 11:1-16; 2 Chronicles 22:10-23:15

At the death of her son, Athaliah made her grab for power. The first thing she did was to destroy the royal family, apparently including her own grandchildren. Only one thing kept her from completely wiping out the line of David. Ahaziah's sister hid his infant son and kept him safe. She was the wife of the good priest Jehoiada.

For six years the vicious daughter of Jezebel held power. During that time she tried to install Baalism as the religion of Judah. Meanwhile Jehoiada the priest was watching over the little prince and getting ready to remove Athaliah. When the time was ripe, Jehoiada carried out his counter-revolution. Now seven years old, Joash was crowned king. When Athaliah came to investigate, she was seized and killed (2 Chronicles 23:1-15).

E. Joash (835-796 B.C.)
2 Kings 12:1-21; 2 Chronicles 23:16–24:27

As long as Jehoiada lived, he had a good influence on Joash. The early part of this young king's reign was exemplary. Among other things, he carried out a refurbishing of the temple, which had fallen into disrepair during Athaliah's usurpation.

When Jehoiada died, however, Joash was easily swayed by evil advisors. Soon the people were abandoning the temple for the Asherah poles and idols. When Zechariah, son of Jehoiada, spoke out against this wickedness, his enemies connived to have him stoned to death by order of the king.

As punishment for this wicked act, God allowed the Arameans or Syrians to invade and plunder Judah. In the conflict Joash was seriously wounded. While he was recovering from his wounds, he was assassinated by some of his own officials.

F. Amaziah (796-767 B.C.)
2 Kings 14:1-20; 2 Chronicles 25:1-28

Amaziah was twenty-five when he came to the throne in the place of his father. We are told that "he did what was right in the eyes of the Lord, but not wholeheartedly" (2 Chronicles 25:2). An example of his weakness is shown when, after a victory over the Edomites, he brought back their idols and then bowed down before them (2 Chronicles 25:14).

Encouraged by his victory over the Edomites, Amaziah made the mistake of challenging Jehoash, king of Israel. Jehoash accepted the challenge, defeated the forces of Judah, and captured Amaziah. Then he marched to Jerusalem, where he tore down long stretches of the wall and took all the gold and silver from the temple. As a result of this humiliating defeat, Amaziah lost the respect of his subjects, some of whom raised a conspiracy against him. He fled from Jerusalem to Lachish to escape his enemies, but they caught him there and killed him.

III. Uzziah to Ahaz

The violence that had earlier become a part of the political scene in the northern kingdom now seemed to be plaguing Judah. The unfaithfulness of some of the kings in allowing pagan worship to be revived undoubtedly contributed to this violence. And once started, violence seemed to beget violence. But with the reign of Uzziah, things took a turn for the better in Judah.

A. Uzziah or Azariah (767-740 B.C.)
2 Kings 15:1-7; 2 Chronicles 26:1-23

Azariah, also known as Uzziah, was only sixteen when he began a co-regency with his father (about 791 B.C.), but he did not become king in his own right until about 767 B.C. He was a good king who brought prosperity to his land. He defeated the Philistines and the Arabs and subjugated the Ammonites. He also embarked on an extensive building program both in Jerusalem and about the countryside. He worked to increase the productivity of the land, "for he loved the soil" (2 Chronicles 26:10). Yet he did not bring about thorough religious reforms because he did not remove the high places (2 Kings 15:4). These were unauthorized places of worship. Idols were worshiped in some of them; in others, the worship of Jehovah was corrupted.

Unfortunately, Uzziah's successes led to pride which in turn led to his downfall. He presumptuously entered the temple to burn incense, something that only the priests could legally do. When the priests tried to warn him, he became quite angry. Because of this arrogant act, God struck him with leprosy. He had to spend the rest of his life in a separate house, and most of his official duties had to be performed by his son, Jotham.

B. Jotham, (740-736 B.C.)
2 Kings 15:32-38; 2 Chronicles 27:1-9

Jotham had to assume the royal responsibilities during the last ten years of his father's reign, and then in 740 B.C. he became king in his own right at Uzziah's death. He generally continued to follow his father's practices. While he supported the worship of the Lord in the temple, he still permitted the high places to remain.

C. Ahaz (736-716 B.C.)
2 Kings 16:1-20; 2 Chronicles 28:1-27

The reign of Ahaz proved to be a disastrous one for Judah. The king soon adopted the pagan religions of his neighbors, even sacrificing his sons in the fire (2 Chronicles 28:3). As a result God allowed him to be chastened by the king of Syria and the king of Israel.

Thinking this coalition was too strong for him, Ahaz turned to the Assyrian king, Tiglath-Pileser, for help. The prophet Isaiah tried to encourage him by informing him that Israel and Syria, depicted as "two smoldering stubs of firewood," would soon be extinguished (Isaiah 7:4). When Ahaz refused to accept the message, Isaiah offered to give him a sign, but the king stubbornly refused to ask for a sign. Then Isaiah proceeded to give to all the house of David a sign from the Lord, that wonderful prophecy of the virgin-born Immanuel (Isaiah 7:14).

The message to Ahaz was that the threat from Israel and Syria would soon be removed. But in their place would come the Assyrians, a far greater threat (Isaiah 7:16, 17). Of course, the prophecy of verse 14 meant something far greater—the promise of the virgin-born Son of God incarnate.

But Ahaz closed his ears to God's word delivered by Isaiah. Instead, he sought and gained Assyria's help. Tiglath-Pileser responded by killing the king of Syria and laying Israel waste. But to gain this aid, Ahaz had to send him treasures stripped from the temple, and Ahaz ended up becoming a vassal of the powerful Assyrian king.

The tragedy of the reign of Ahaz reminds us that the wealth and virtue of a nation can quickly be squandered by one willful and wicked leader.

Later History of Judah

End of Northern Kingdom of Israel About 722 B.C.

Kings of Judah	*Prophets*
Ahaz 736-716	
Hezekiah 716-687	
Manasseh 687-642	
Amon 642-640	Nahum 640
Josiah 640-609	Zephaniah 630-625
Jehoahaz 609	Jeremiah 628-585
Jehoiakim 609-597	Habakkuk 612-606

First Captives to Babylon	Daniel 606-534
Jehoiachin 597	
Zedekiah 597-586	Ezekiel 593-571

Jerusalem Destroyed 586

Captivity in Babylon 586-536	
Return From Babylon 536	Haggai 520
Temple Completed 516	Zechariah 520
Esther in Persia 479	
Ezra in Judah 458-457	
Nehemiah in Judah 445-444	Malachi 430

End of Old Testament About 430 B.C.

Fall of the Southern Kingdom (716-586 B.C.)

2 Kings 18:1—25:30; 2 Chronicles 29:1—36:23

Introduction

The tragic reign of Ahaz brought Judah to the brink of disaster. He corrupted his people religiously by turning to the worship of pagan idols, and he entered a political alliance with Assyria that reduced Judah to the status of a vassal.

I. Hezekiah, Manasseh, Amon

A. Hezekiah (716-687 B.C.)
2 Kings 18:1–20:21; 2 Chronicles 29:1–32:33

Many scholars date the beginning of Hezekiah's reign about 730 B.C. This synchronizes with the information given in 2 Kings 18:1, 9, 10, but it is likely that this date marked the beginning of his co-regency with his father, and that he became king in his own right in 716 B.C.

The times were not promising when Hezekiah came to the throne. The demands of the Assyrians, who had already destroyed Syria and Israel, became even more pressing. Judah lacked the strength to resist them. But this good king had two things in his favor—he had a strong faith in God and he had the counsel of the trusted prophet Isaiah.

Among the first things he did upon taking office was to remove the high places and cut down the Asherah poles. Then he defeated the Philistines and rebelled against the Assyrian overlords. Sennacherib, who was now the Assyrian monarch, responded by attacking and capturing all the fortified cities of Judah. Realizing that he had gone too far too fast, Hezekiah sued for peace. It cost him all the gold and silver he could scrape up. An inscription of Sennacherib confirms that Hezekiah paid this tribute. But in spite of the tribute, the Assyrian king was not satisfied. Perhaps he was afraid to leave intact such a strong fortification as Jerusalem, and so he laid siege to the city. On the Taylor Cylinder, discovered at the site of ancient Nineveh, Sennacherib boasts about how he shut Hezekiah up in Jerusalem "like a bird in a cage." Yet he makes no mention of actually taking the city—and for good reason!

When Hezekiah realized his plight, he went into the temple and prayed. Isaiah then sent the king an encouraging word: The Lord assured him that the king of Assyria would "not enter this city or shoot an arrow here" (2 Kings 19:32). God then proceeded to answer Hezekiah's prayer in a most dramatic fashion. During the night the angel of the Lord visited the Assyrian camp and left a hundred and eighty-five thousand dead men behind. Sennacherib's record does not mention that, but he would hardly be expected to report such a catastrophe. However, we know that he returned to Assyria and never again bothered Judah. Before long he was assassinated by two of his sons.

Following his successful resistance of Sennacherib, Hezekiah received the acclaim of the nations about him (2 Chronicles 32:23). Under his wise leadership, Judah prospered and the people were brought back to the worship of the true God. He strengthened the defense of Jerusalem by cutting a tunnel nearly eighteen hundred feet through solid rock from the spring of Gihon to the pool of Siloam. This conduit, which insured a water supply inside the city during siege, can still be seen today. Following his long and fruitful life, Hezekiah was buried with honors.

B. Manasseh (687-642 B.C.)
2 Kings 21:1-18; 2 Chronicles 33:1-20

Manasseh was only twelve years old when he became king. His long reign was one of the most tragic in Judah's history. His father had brought a great spiritual revival to the land, but Manasseh succeeded in destroying all that his father had accomplished. He rebuilt the high places Hezekiah had destroyed. He erected altars to Baal and made an Asherah pole. In the temple court he built altars to "the starry hosts." He even sacrificed his own son in the fire.

The Lord spoke to Manasseh, but the willful king refused to heed the warning. And so God brought against Manasseh the king of Assyria, who took him back to Babylon as a prisoner. This painful experience jarred Manasseh to his senses and brought him to repentance. The Lord allowed him to return to Judah and repair the walls of Jerusalem. He also got rid of the foreign gods and the altars he had built in Jerusalem, and he restored the altars of the Lord; but apparently his reform efforts came too late. The people "continued to sacrifice at the high places" (2 Chronicles 33:17). The life of Manasseh illustrates how the effects of wicked deeds can never be completely removed, even when the sinner repents and does his best to make amends.

C. Amon (642-640 B.C.)
2 Kings 21:19-26; 2 Chronicles 33:21-25
In Amon's case it was "like father, like son," for he followed in his father's footsteps and did evil in the eyes of God. Manasseh's reforms failed to influence his son. When he was confronted with his sins, he refused to humble himself before God.

After a reign of only two years, some of Amon's officials conspired against him and murdered him. The plotters in turn were killed by the people.

II. Josiah to Zedekiah
A. Josiah (640-609 B.C.)
2 Kings 22:1–23:30; 2 Chronicles 34:1–35:27
As we examine the lives of the kings of Judah, we are struck by the fact that often a good king produced a bad son. Fortunately, the reverse was often true—a bad king produced a good son. Such was the case of Josiah. His father and grandfather before him had been exceedingly wicked. Yet Josiah was zealous for God and carried out extensive reforms within his kingdom.

Josiah was only eight when he became king. Wise counselors directed the nation until he came of age. When he was sixteen, he began earnestly to serve the Lord. Four years later he began to purge the land of the high places, Asherah poles, and idols. He destroyed the altars of Baal and even burned the bones of the pagan priests on their altars. His reforming zeal was not confined to Judah, but he extended his efforts into Ephraim, Manasseh, and Simeon as far as Naphtali. He was able to do this because the power of Assyria apparently was waning in the area.

When he was twenty-six, Josiah launched a campaign to repair the temple. Collections for this repair work were gathered from the scattered tribes of the north as well as from the people of Judah. From the description of the work, it would seem that the temple had been seriously neglected for many years.

In the midst of this repair work in 621 B.C., a dramatic discovery was made. Hilkiah, the high priest, found the Book of the Law. Whether it had been left forgotten in some remote corner of the temple or whether it had been placed in the cornerstone of the temple, we are not told. The book was immediately taken to the king and read to him. Upon hearing the words, the king was moved to remorse because he realized that the law had been neglected for many years. He then asked Hilkiah to go before the Lord in prayer to discover what they should do.

Hilkiah sought out Huldah, who was recognized as a prophetess of God. Her word was a sobering message indeed. Because the law had been neglected, God's anger would be poured out upon them. Yet because Josiah had humbled himself when the law was found, God would spare him this retribution. Disaster would come later, to ungodly rulers.

Josiah's next action was to call together the leaders and the people in the temple. There he read to them all the words of the Book of the Covenant and led them in a renewing of their covenant with God. After this, Josiah led the people to observe the Passover. It seems that the Passover had not been observed or at least had not been observed properly for many generations, all the way back to the time of Samuel (2 Chronicles 35:18).

Josiah's glorious reign was cut short when he unwisely allowed himself to become involved in a military action against the pharaoh of Egypt. Pharaoh Neco passed Palestine on his way to aid the Assyrian king against the Babylonians and Medes. For some reason, Josiah felt obligated to try to stop him. The spot at which he chose to meet the pharaoh was Megiddo, often identified with Armageddon. During the battle (dated about 609 B.C.), Josiah was mortally wounded by an arrow. He died in Jerusalem, where he was buried with honor. We are told that Jeremiah composed laments for Josiah that were sung for many years and became a tradition among the people (2 Chronicles 35:25).

B. Jehoahaz (609 B.C.)
2 Kings 23:31-34; 2 Chronicles 36:1-4

Josiah was succeeded by his son, Jehoahaz. His reign was brief indeed—only three months—for he was seized by Pharaoh Neco and taken as a prisoner to Egypt, where he died. Perhaps it was just as well for Judah's sake that his reign was short, for we are told that "he did evil in the eyes of the Lord."

C. Jehoiakim (609-597)
2 Kings 23:34–24:6; 2 Chronicles 36:4-8

Following Jehoahaz's deportation to Egypt, the pharaoh placed the king's brother, Eliakim, on the throne as a puppet and changed his name to Jehoiakim. During his eleven-year reign, he did evil in the eyes of the Lord. In the meantime a new power had arisen in Mesopotamia. The Babylonians and their allies had captured and destroyed Nineveh in 612 B.C. Then the Babylonian king, Nebuchadnezzar, turned his attention to the lands once dominated by Assyria. It appears that the first incursion of Nebuchadnezzar into Judah came in 606 B.C. At the time he sent back to Babylon as hostages some of the sons of the prominent people in Jerusalem. Among them were Daniel and some of his friends (Daniel 1:1-7).

Later Nebuchadnezzar withdrew temporarily from the west, and Jehoiakim began to entertain the idea of throwing off the Babylonian yoke. Jeremiah, a prophet who had been called during the reign of Josiah, tried to warn the king not to attempt such action, but to turn from his wicked ways before God sent judgment upon him. Jeremiah dictated the messages God had given him, and his scribe Baruch saw that the scroll of them got to the king. The king not only rejected the message; he contemptuously cut up the scroll and cast it into the fire (Jeremiah 36:1-26).

Jehoiakim's days were numbered, however. Before long (598 B.C.) Nebuchadnezzar returned to Judah. Apparently Jehoiakim died or was assassinated about that time, so the next king was the one who had to face the invader.

D. Jehoiachin (597 B.C.)
2 Kings 24:8-17; 2 Chronicles 36:9, 10

Jehoiakim was succeeded by his son, Jehoiachin, who was only eighteen when he came to the throne. He reigned only three months, for he wisely surrendered instead of trying to fight off the forces of Babylon. Nebuchadnezzar had him brought to Babylonia, along with "articles of value from the temple." Many others were deported to Babylonia at this time, including the prophet Ezekiel. Later, when Evil-Merodach became king of Babylonia, he released Jehoiachin from prison and gave him a place of honor in his kingdom; but he did not allow him to return to Judah and become king again (2 Kings 25:27-30).

E. Zedekiah (597-586 B.C.)
2 Kings 24:17–25:21; 2 Chronicles 36:11-20

After deposing Jehoiachin, Nebuchadnezzar placed Mattaniah, Jehoiachin's uncle, on the throne, and changed his name to Zedekiah. Zedekiah proved to be a weak and vacillating ruler. Some of his advisors urged him to seek support from Egypt, even though Jeremiah urged him to submit to Babylonia. False prophets kept the people's hopes high for an early return of the captives who had been taken to Babylonia. Jeremiah, on the other hand, urged the people to prepare for a long captivity (Jeremiah 29:1-10).

Zedekiah finally heeded the advice of his pro-Egyptian advisors and revolted against Nebuchadnezzar. The decision was a tragic blunder, for the Babylonian army was soon entrenched around Jerusalem. After a siege of several months, Nebuchadnezzar's forces breeched the walls (586 B.C.). Zedekiah escaped from the city, but was finally captured near Jericho. Angered by his revolt, Nebuchadnezzar did not deal gently with him. The sons of Zedekiah were killed before him, and then his own eyes were put out and he was taken to Babylon in chains.

In the meantime, the Babylonian troops were busy pillaging Jerusalem. Its treasures were dismantled and sent back to Babylon; most of its buildings, including the temple, were burned; and its massive walls were torn down. Many captives, especially the leading citizens, were deported to Babylon. Only the poorest people were left to till the soil (2 Kings 25:11, 12). Judgment had finally come to Judah!

Gedaliah was appointed governor over the desolated land, but still peace had not come. A band of extremists succeeded in assassinating Gedaliah and some of his officers. Many of the other citizens, fearing Nebuchadnezzar's revenge, fled to Egypt, taking with them the prophet Jeremiah. The long discouraging exile had begun (2 Kings 25:22-26; Jeremiah 40:1—44:30).

The Exile and Return

Ezekiel, Daniel, Ezra, Nehemiah, Esther

I. The Exile (Jeremiah 39—44)

The destruction of Jerusalem by the forces of Nebuchadnezzar in 586 B.C. left Judah a shattered nation. Her treasures had been carried off to Babylon; her capital and many of her other cities had been destroyed; most of her leaders had either been taken to Babylonia as captives or had fled to Egypt for refuge. Only the poorest people were left. Without leadership or resources, their hopes of restoring their land must have been slight indeed. It would not have been at all surprising if the Jews after this crushing defeat had simply disappeared from history. Many other peoples under similar circumstances have lost their identity and ceased to exist as distinct peoples, but God had a purpose for the Jews. Because they were a part of His plan, He watched over them and cared for them even in these dire straits.

A. The Historical Situation (Psalm 137)

The Bible tells us very little about the Jews during their captivity. Interestingly, the term *Jew* did not come into wide usage until the time of the exile. Originally it may have been used to designate the people of the tribe of Judah, but later it was applied to all of the descendants of Israel, as it is today. A member of any of the twelve tribes is called a Jew.

The Neo-Babylonian Empire, which was responsible for the exile of the Jews, was vast, stretching from Egypt to Mesopotamia. Under Nebuchadnezzar the city of Babylon became a beautiful and thriving metropolis. No doubt much of the construction was carried out by prisoners of war brought in from foreign lands, and the city was enhanced by the wealth confiscated from the conquered territories.

B. Ezekiel *(Ezekiel)*

Ezekiel was carried off when the Babylonians captured Jerusalem in 597 B.C. He was settled with some of the other exiles along the Kebar River, or Chebar, as the name is spelled in the King James Version. This was probably a canal in the elaborate irrigation system the Babylonians had developed between the Tigris and Euphrates Rivers. It was there that Ezekiel received his call to minister to his fellow exiles. His task was not an easy one. On the one hand, he had to bring encouragement to a defeated and disheartened people. On the other, he had to bring them to realize that they needed to repent of their sins, which had caused them to be carried into captivity. Until Jerusalem fell, he had to pronounce doom upon the city and to counter the optimistic predictions of false prophets who promised an early return of the exiles to Judah. When Jerusalem was destroyed in 586 B.C., Ezekiel changed his message and encouraged the people to look forward to their eventual return, although that return was many years in the future.

C. Daniel *(Daniel)*

Daniel was carried off as a hostage in 606 B.C. in Nebuchadnezzar's first campaign against Jerusalem. Daniel's ministry, unlike that of Ezekiel, was not to his own people in exile but to the rulers who were their conquerors. During his long ministry, he brought God's prophetic message to the Babylonian rulers Nebuchadnezzar and Belshazzar, and later to the Persian rulers, Darius and Cyrus.

II. The Return *(Ezra 1-6)*

A. The Persian Empire *(Ezra 1:1-11)*

The Neo-Babylonian Empire rose quickly to a position of power, and just as quickly it collapsed. Even as Nebuchadnezzar was creating his empire, the Medes and Persians to the north and east were also organizing and developing. In 539 B.C., the Persians, led by Cyrus the Great, launched a campaign against Babylonia. Belshazzar, the Babylonian king, felt quite secure behind the high, thick walls of his city. The book of Daniel tells of the swift destruction that overwhelmed him in the midst of his revelries (Daniel 5).

Cyrus' conquests and those of his successors soon included Syria, Palestine, and Egypt. Once he had conquered what had been the Neo-babylonian Empire, he turned his attention to organizing this vast territory so that he could govern it more efficiently. Cyrus took a generous attitude toward the Jewish exiles and soon arranged for them to return to Palestine if they wanted to. In anticipating Cyrus' benevolence toward the Jews, the prophet Isaiah a century and a half earlier had indicated that the Persian king was God's "shepherd" (Isaiah 44:28) and God's "anointed" (Isaiah 45:1) to accomplish His purpose.

B. The First Returnees *(Ezra 2:1–3:6)*

In 536 B.C. the first of the exiles returned to Judah, carrying with them a decree from Cyrus authorizing the rebuilding of the temple. Since after seventy years of captivity many of the Jews had become permanently settled in Babylonia, only about fifty thousand made their way back to their homeland. Their leader was Zerubbabel (Ezra 3:2), who encouraged them to build an altar to God as soon as they arrived. On the first day of the seventh month they were able to begin offering burnt offerings to the Lord (Ezra 3:6).

C. The Rebuilding of the Temple *(Ezra 3:7–6:22)*

During the second year of their return, the exiles laid the foundation for the second temple. However, the work soon met with opposition from the Samaritans. Cyrus had specifically approved the project, but the Samaritans persuaded a later king to order it stopped. For some years there was no more work on the unfinished building.

The prophets Haggai and Zechariah were both moved by the Lord to speak out and arouse the people to resume their building activities. By their preaching the apathy was overcome, and the people turned again to rebuilding the temple in 520 B.C. The encouragement of these two prophets was adequate to keep them at the task, and in about four years the temple was completed.

The king who had forbidden it now was gone, and the new king supported the project.

Finally the day came when the temple was completed. This certainly must rank as one of the most glorious days in the history of Judah. Hundreds of animals were sacrificed for the occasion. Then a joyous Passover was celebrated by those who had returned from exile. It was indeed commendable that these impoverished people were able to accomplish so much.

III. The Work of Ezra *(Ezra 7–10)*

More than fifty years passed between the dedication of the temple and the arrival of Ezra in 458 B.C. During this time the people had become dispirited. They had not prospered as many of them had hoped to, and by intermarrying with other peoples they had compromised their earlier resolve to remain separate from their neighbors. Further, the walls of Jerusalem had not been rebuilt, and the Jews were subject to harassment and attack.

A. Ezra's Return to Jerusalem *(Ezra 7, 8)*

Ezra was a pious Levite living in Babylon, who shared with some of his neighbors the desire to migrate to Judah. When Ezra asked for permission to go, King Artaxerxes not only gave it, but also sent with him offerings to provide for sacrifices in the temple. Ezra was also authorized to appoint judges and magistrates and to teach the law of God.

About eighteen hundred men along with their families volunteered to return with Ezra (Ezra 8:1-20). After fasting, they humbled themselves before God and asked Him for a safe journey. After a trip of several months, they arrived in Jerusalem where they presented their treasures in the temple.

B. Ezra's Reforms *(Ezra 9, 10)*

Ezra soon turned his attention to carrying out the reforms he felt were needed. One of the most serious problems he saw was that of intermarriage with people of non-Jewish tribes. He challenged the Jews to set aside these marriages. Some resisted his suggestion, but most of the people supported him. Special judges were set up to carry out the divorces in a proper manner. No doubt this action stirred up resentment among the non-Jewish tribes about them, but Ezra was determined to maintain the purity of his people at any cost.

IV. The Work of Nehemiah *(Nehemiah 1–13)*

The opening of the book of Nehemiah finds him in Susa, an important city in Persia. He was "cupbearer to the king" (Nehemiah 1:11), a very responsible officer in the service of King Artaxerxes. Then word came that things were not going well in Jerusalem. The temple had been completed seventy years earlier. About thirteen years had passed since Ezra had instituted his reforms. But among the other tribes in Palestine the Jews were in disgrace because the walls of Jerusalem had never been rebuilt.

A. Nehemiah's Return *(Nehemiah 2)*

This sad news placed a heavy burden on Nehemiah's heart, and it showed so plainly in his countenance that the king noticed it and inquired about it. When Artaxerxes learned the cause of Nehemiah's problem, he generously offered him the opportunity to return to Jerusalem. Not only that, but the king appointed him governor of the Jews and sent him with letters of safe conduct and permission to cut timbers from the king's forest.

It was about 445 B.C. when Nehemiah arrived in Jerusalem. With a few men he inspected the ruined walls at night to get some idea of the kind of job that lay before him. Most of the stones lay where they had fallen when the Babylonians had crushed the city a hundred and forty years before. When his inspection tour was completed, Nehemiah met with the leaders and challenged them to start rebuilding. They responded enthusiastically.

B. Rebuilding the Walls *(Nehemiah 3–6)*

When the enemies learned of Nehemiah's plan, they ridiculed it. But nothing they could say could affect his resolve. The rebuilding began, with different groups working in different places. When progress on the wall became obvious, Sanballat and other enemies tried several strategems to get the work stopped. Finally they plotted a military attack on the unfinished walls. Word of their plan leaked out, however. Nehemiah armed the workers and posted guards with swords, spears, and bows. Deprived of the advantage of surprise, the enemies abandoned their plan.

So the enemies were thwarted, the people worked enthusiastically, and the walls were finished in only fifty-two days. There was great rejoicing then, and the enemies "lost their self-confidence, because they realized that this work had been done with the help of our God" (Nehemiah 6:16).

Besides rebuilding the walls, Nehemiah promptly ordered reforms that helped the poor (Nehemiah 5). It seems probable that Ezra had gone back to Persia after the reformation he had brought about thirteen years before Nehemiah came. But now he was in Jerusalem again, teaching the law of God and supporting the new governor in his reforms (Nehemiah 8—10).

C. Nehemiah's Policies *(Nehemiah 11–13)*
Nehemiah set out to strengthen Jerusalem by bringing in more residents, though most of the people still lived in the areas where their ancestors had lived centuries before.

After some time Nehemiah went back to Persia. We are not told how long he stayed, but it was long enough for the people to become lax again in keeping the law. Upon his return, Nehemiah dealt with the offenders. He insisted on the tithes and offerings needed for upkeep of the temple. He stressed Sabbath observance and ordered the gates of the city closed on the Sabbath so that merchants could not enter the city on that day. He also strongly opposed marriage between Jews and their non-Jewish neighbors.

It would be hard to overestimate the value of Nehemiah's contribution to the Jewish nation. He gave up a comfortable job with Artaxerxes to help his own people when they needed it. By encouraging them to rebuild the walls of Jerusalem, he made them able to defend themselves; and by leading them in religious and social reforms, he gave them a sense of identity and mission.

V. The Story of Esther *(Esther 1–10)*
Not all of the Jews returned to Palestine. Many remained in Persia and Babylonia. In later generations many of them probably abandoned their Jewish faith and lost their identity as Jews, but some held fast to the convictions of their ancestors. Two such persons living in Persia during the reign of Xerxes were Mordecai and his cousin, Esther, whom Mordecai had reared because her parents were dead. Xerxes is called Ahasuerus in the King James Version. He ruled about 485-465 B.C.

A. Esther Becomes Queen *(Esther 1, 2)*
Xerxes became unhappy with his queen, Vashti, and had her deposed. Then he launched a beauty contest to find a successor. Esther won the king's approval and became his new queen. But

before long, Esther and all the Jews faced a serious threat. Haman, who bitterly despised Mordecai, got a royal decree from Xerxes to kill all Jews. Neither Haman nor the king knew of Mordecai's relationship with the new queen.

B. The Plot Against the Jews *(Esther 3–9)*

Mordecai, once he learned of the plot, prevailed upon Esther to use her influence with the king to save her people. At considerable risk to herself, Esther came before the king to ask him to attend a banquet that she had prepared. Haman was also invited to this banquet. Later that night the king could not sleep, and so he began to read some old records. There he found that he had not properly rewarded Mordecai for reporting a plot against the king's life.

At another banquet Esther revealed Haman's plot against the Jews. The king in his anger ordered Haman hanged on the very gallows he had erected to execute Mordecai. By Persian law the King's decree could not be changed, but the king issued a second decree that brought a massacre of the Jew's enemies instead of the Jews.

As a result of Esther's heroic effort to save her people, a special festival was begun—Purim, which is celebrated on the fourteenth and fifteenth of Adar, corresponding to our February—March. Persecutions of the Jews since Esther's day have continued to make the observance of Purim meaningful.

The Songs and Literature of a Nation

Job, Psalms, Proverbs, Ecclesiastes, Song of Solomon

Several of the previous chapters have dealt with the history of the Hebrew nation. But a bare recounting of history does not do justice to these people, nor does it exhaust the wealth of the Old Testament revelation. Some of the most helpful and best loved portions of the Old Testament are found in the poetical books—Job, Psalms, Proverbs, Ecclesiastes, and the Song of Solomon.

I. The Book of Job

The book of Job deals with a universal human problem—the problem of suffering. The answer that it suggests is not a scientific nor a philosophical answer, but rather a religious answer, an answer that must ultimately be accepted by faith.

A. Author, Date, and Setting

We have no information about who the author of the book of Job was. Nor, for that matter, is it possible to assign it a definite date. The setting is "the land of Uz," which was probably located south and east of Palestine, near Edom or northwestern Arabia. The setting seems to be rural in an area where there were both pasture lands and plowed fields. The life-style was relatively simple and unhurried. From these circumstances many suppose Job lived at about the time of Abraham, which was about 2000 B.C.

B. The Narrative (Job 1, 2)

The book opens with Job "blameless and upright," in the prime of life, and enjoying the blessings God has showered upon him. He has three daughters and seven sons, and he possesses great numbers of sheep, camels, oxen, and donkeys attended by numerous servants.

The scene changes, and we are ushered into the presence of the Lord. There we see the angels coming before Him. Into this Heavenly gathering stalks Satan, seeking as always to antagonize God. On this occasion, however, God has a response—Job, a man who fears God and shuns evil. But Satan does not lack for an answer. "Does Job fear God for nothing?" he sneers. "Have you not put a hedge around him and his household . . . and blessed the work of his hands?" (Job 1:9, 10).

In other words, Satan suggests that Job serves God only because it is profitable. "Strike everything he has, and he will surely curse you to your face," he challenges. God rises to the challenge and gives Satan permission to take from Job his family and possessions. As a result, a series of disasters befalls Job. He loses his children and his flocks. Yet his faith remains unshakable.

Satan is persistent. Once more he comes before the Lord, still cynical about Job. This time he requests that God allow him to afflict Job physically. As a result, Job is covered with painful sores from head to foot. He is in such agony that he sits on a heap of ashes and scrapes his sores with a piece of broken pottery. The prologue ends with Job in such misery that even his wife urges him to curse God and die. Still, through all of this Job "did not sin in what he said" (Job 2:10).

C. The Theological Problem

After the lapse of some time during which Job's physical condition worsens, he is visited by three friends—Eliphaz, Bildad, and Zophar—who come from some distance to offer him consolation. But their consolation soon turns to criticism. The orthodox view of the time is that suffering comes as a result of God's displeasure. Since Job is not guilty of any evident sin that would require such punishment, his friends accuse him of harboring some terrible secret sin. Job vehemently denies their accusations, but they persist. In the midst of this discussion Job expresses his profound faith not only in the integrity of God but in life after death. "If a man dies, will he live again?'' he asks (Job 14:14). Then in 19:25, 26 he answers, ''I know that my Redeemer lives. . . . And after my skin has been destroyed, yet in my flesh I will see God.''

After his friends spend their vehemence upon him, another man, Elihu, enters the discussion (Job 32:2ff). He continues the indictment of Job until he is interrupted by the Lord, who speaks out of the storm.

God asks a series of pointed questions that show up the ignorance of Job and his friends and demonstrate His divine wisdom. Job is overwhelmed by this and humbly acknowledges his own ignorance, repenting in ''dust and ashes.'' The book concludes by recounting the blessings the Lord pours out upon Job in his later years. He lives many fruitful years and dies in blessed peace.

D. The Practical Application

The book of Job does not give us a complete answer to the problem of suffering. Indeed, it suggests that often there is no answer, at least none that can be known or understood by man. Sin certainly does produce a great deal of suffering, but beyond this is much suffering for which we can give no logical explanation. The message of Job is that our suffering may arise as a part of God's cosmic strategy that we will never be able to understand in this life. This knowledge can lead us to the kind of faith that caused Job to cry out, ''I know that my Redeemer lives!''

II. Psalms, the Hebrew Hymnal

The Hebrew title for Psalms means ''Book of praises.'' This is fitting, for many of the psalms have the praise of God as their theme.

A. Date and Authorship

The psalms were written and gradually brought together as one book over a period of a thousand years. Psalm 90 is ascribed to Moses, and other psalms bear a striking resemblance to songs found among the Ras Shamra tablets that date back to the Mosaic period. Most of the psalms were written during the time when the Hebrew kingdom was flourishing. Others reflect conditions that prevailed during the exile (102, 137) and even after (85, 126). We have no way of knowing when the various psalms were finally collected in one book.

Nearly half of the psalms are ascribed to David. Some are

credited to Asaph (50, 73-83), while the sons of Korah are credited with several others (42-49, 84, 85, 87). Some scholars attribute a few psalms to the prophet Jeremiah. About one-third of the psalms are anonymous.

B. Hebrew Poetry

Hebrew poetry is different from English poetry. It does not rhyme, nor does it have meter as we use meter in English. It is marked by vivid and picturesque langauge, and many Hebrew words are used almost exclusively in poetry.

Another quality of Hebrew poetry is called parallelism. In *synonymous parallelism* the same idea is expressed in different words. For example, the first part of Psalm 8:4 reads, "What is man that you are mindful of him?" The second part of the verse, almost like an echo, repeats the same idea: "the son of man that you care for him?"

In *antithetic parallelism,* the second part of the verse is the opposite of the first. See Psalm 34:10: "The lions may grow weak and hungry, but those who seek the Lord lack no good thing."

In *synthetic parallelism* the thought pattern moves toward a climax with each succeeding line adding to the previous lines. Note Psalm 19:8, 9: "The precepts of the Lord are right, giving joy to the heart. The commands of the Lord are radiant, giving light to the eyes. The fear of the Lord is pure, enduring forever. The ordinances of the Lord are sure and altogether righteous."

C. The Organization of the Book of Psalms

The psalms are divided into five divisions or books. The first division includes Psalms 1-41; the second division, Psalms 42-72; the third, Psalms 73-89; the fourth, Psalms 90-106; and the fifth, Psalms 107-150. Within these major divisions are other groupings. Psalms 120-134, for example, are called "Psalms of Ascents," or "Songs of Degrees." Many scholars believe that these psalms were sung by the pilgrims as they traveled to Jerusalem for the three great feasts. Another group (93-100) praises the Lord for His virtues and His deeds. Psalms 145-150 close the book with songs of praise.

D. Some Themes in the Book of Psalms

Many of the psalms face squarely the fact that man is a sinner. In some, man confesses his sins; in others he seeks forgiveness;

in still others he finds forgiveness and joy from God. Some (Psalms 6, 32, 38, 51, 102, 130, 143) have been called "Penetential Psalms" because they show man repenting and seeking forgiveness. Psalm 51 is David's cry for forgiveness after his sin with Bathsheba. Psalm 32 follows some time later, when David has begun to taste the sweet joy of forgiveness.

Some psalms (among them 35, 69, 109) pose a serious problem to sensitive Christians because of the strong language that the writers use against their enemies. Their cries for bloody revenge seem to contradict the teachings of Jesus that we ought to forgive our enemies. Many students have noted that these imprecatory psalms, as they are sometimes called, reflect a culture and standards quite different from our own. Others remind us that ancient writers often resorted to extreme exaggeration for the purpose of emphasis. This rhetoric seems quite harsh to us because we are inclined to take it literally, but the ancients understood it for what it really was. More important, we need to understand that the psalmist is not just crying out for vengeance on his personal enemies, but on the enemies of God. The New Testament also is quite plain about God's vengeance (Matthew 3:11, 12; 11:20-24; 13:40-42; 25:41-46; Luke 19:41-44; Romans 12:19; 2 Thessalonians 1:5-10; Hebrews 10:26-31; Jude 5-7; Revelation 20:11-15).

One of the most important themes of the Psalms is prophecy of the coming Messiah. Psalm 22 tells of Jesus' suffering and death. Jesus himself on the cross quoted its opening words: "My God, my God, why have you forsaken me?" His words, "I thirst," reflect a Messianic prediction found in Psalm 69:21. John 19:36 quotes Psalm 34:20 in referring to the fact that none of Christ's bones would be broken in the crucifixion.

Other psalms (2 and 110) refer to the Messiah as a conquering king. Others point out the expansive nature of His kingdom. Psalms 47, 67, 96-100, and 117 indicate that redemption is for all people, "Clap your hands, all you nations" begins Psalm 47. "May your ways be known on earth, your salvation among all nations," reads Psalm 67.

For most people the psalms are best known and loved as a source of inspiration and hope. Perhaps the most memorized passage in the whole Bible is the twenty-third Psalm. Its words of hope, couched in terms of the pastoral life so familiar to David, have brought comfort to countless millions and will continue their ministry till the end of time.

III. Proverbs

The books of Proverbs, Ecclesiastes, and the Song of Solomon are often called the Wisdom Literature of the Old Testament. Many attribute all three books to Solomon and suggest that he wrote the Song of Solomon as a young man, Proverbs in his middle years, and Ecclesiastes as an old man.

First Kings 4:32 tells us that Solomon "spoke three thousand proverbs." Apparently we have many of these in the book of Proverbs. Some are brief sayings that set forth gems of practical wisdom, but there are other forms of ethical statements.

Chapters 1—9 serve as an introduction to the whole book, presenting the concept of Wisdom and setting forth the spiritual attitude of one who properly receives Wisdom. The exhortations are couched in terms that a father might use in addressing "my son" or "my sons." The theme for the whole book is located in 1:7: "The fear of the Lord is the beginning of knowledge, but fools despise wisdom and discipline."

The second section is chapters 10:1—22:16. Like the first, it has the heading, "the proverbs of Solomon." It abounds in two-line proverbs employing parallelism, either synonymous or antithetical. In each verse the first line states a proposition. Then the second line makes a statement that either repeats the first line in different words or contrasts with it. Many of these contrasts are familiar to us: "A wise son brings joy to his father, but a foolish son grief to his mother" (10:1); "Better a meal of vegetables where there is love, than a fattened calf with hatred" (15:17); "Righteousness exalts a nation, but sin is a disgrace to any people" (14:34); "A gentle answer turns away wrath, but a harsh word stirs up anger" (15:1) and "There is a way that seems right to a man, but in the end it leads to death (14:12).

A short section (22:17—24:22) is well described as sayings of the wise, as is the shorter section that follows it (24:23-34). Perhaps the best-known verses from these sections are those that deal with the use of wine (23:29-35). The advice is just as good today as when Solomon uttered it nearly three thousand years ago: "Do not gaze at wine when it is red, when it sparkles in the cup, when it goes down smoothly! In the end it bites like a snake and poisons like a viper" (23:31, 32).

The next section (chapters 25—29) presents more proverbs of Solomon. This is followed by "Sayings of Agur" (chapter 30) and "Sayings of King Lemuel" (chapter 31). The book closes with a poem extolling the virtues of a worthy woman (31:10-31). We most frequently hear these words on Mother's Day, but they are certainly applicable every day of the year.

IV. Ecclesiastes

The writer of this book calls himself "son of David, king in Jerusalem," which leads us to conclude that the author is none other than Solomon, although many scholars think it comes from a later time. The key word of the book is "vanity," or "meaningless," as the New International Version has it. This pessimistic conclusion very well fits the life of Solomon, who had all kinds of experiences but whose life seemed to end in disappointment.

The writer was a man who had tried almost everything in his search for satisfaction. He had tried wisdom (1:16-18) but he had found that "with much wisdom comes much sorrow." He had tried pleasure. He had undertaken great projects—building houses, planting vineyards, and building gardens and parks. He had amassed great wealth. Yet all of these were meaningless.

From his vantage point of years of experience, perhaps near the end of his life, he could look back and conclude that man's efforts to find satisfaction in the things of this world are doomed to failure. Even study and contemplation were useless as he stated, "Of making many books there is no end, and much study wearies the body" (12:12).

Yet his life was not totally wasted, for his experience allowed him to hand down some advice that can be helpful to all of us. "Remember your Creator in the days of your youth" is his admonition (12:1). "Fear God and keep his commandments, for this is the whole duty of man. For God will bring every deed into judgment, including every hidden thing, whether it is good or evil" (12:13, 14). Such advice is certainly most appropriate for the "me" generation that seeks satisfaction only in the gratification of its own desires and rejects any responsibility to God or its fellow men.

V. The Song of Solomon

This book, also known as Song of Songs and Canticles, has been a source of controversy for centuries. Not only has its authorship been questioned, but it has been subjected to various types of interpretation. Traditionally the book has been ascribed to Solomon, and there are many things within it to support this.

One interpretation views this work literally as a beautiful love poem that may have been quoted at weddings. One version of this position sees the poem as a dialogue between a lover and his beloved as they prepare for their coming marriage.

Early Christian commentators found the erotic language of the poem offensive if taken literally. They sought to avoid this by denying that it had any historical basis whatever and by interpreting it allegorically, finding in the colorful language an expression of Christ's love for His church. Some of these interpretations were strained to the point of being ridiculous.

Some modern commentators take a third approach. They regard the book as a love poem that is not offensive, but is a wholesome expression of physical love between a man and his intended bride. At the same time, they insist that it projects moral truths that go beyond this. They feel that this is an Old Testament picture of God's love for His children, just as the New Testament uses the figure of the church as the bride of Christ. Approached in this way, the book can be a source of spiritual edification even though commentators do not agree about all the details of interpretation.

The Prophets

Isaiah—Malachi

The ancient Hebrew prophets were spokesmen for God: that is, they brought God's message to the people. They differed from modern preachers in at least one important way—they were "seers." Through divine inspiration they were given the power to see things or gain insights beyond those that man may naturally receive. Many persons in the Old Testament period met those qualifications and were actually called prophets. Among these were Abraham (Genesis 20:7), Moses (Deuteronomy 34:10), Deborah (Judges 4:4), and Samuel (1 Samuel 3:19, 20). From Samuel's time on we begin to read of groups of prophets who were sometimes referred to as "sons of prophets" (1 Samuel 10:5; 19:19, 20; 1 Kings 18:4; 20:35). Nathan, that stern prophet of righteousness, was sent by God to rebuke King David (2 Samuel 12:1-14). In the ninth century the great prophets Elijah, Elisha, and Micaiah faithfully served Jehovah.

Then in the eighth century there appeared the first of the writing prophets, sometimes called canonical prophets because their writings make up a major division of the Old Testament. These prophetic books are sometimes divided into two groups—the major prophets (Isaiah, Jeremiah, Ezekiel, and Daniel) and the minor prophets (Hosea to Malachi). This division is based on the length of their books—the books of the major prophets are longer. For this study it seems more appropriate to discuss the prophets and their work chronologically under four periods: the Assyrian, the Babylonian, the Exilic, and the Post-Exilic.

I. The Assyrian Period (about 800-612 B.C.)

Six prophets, whose ministries were quite varied, will be considered during this period of about two hundred years.

A. Joel (about 800 B.C.)

Scholars are not in agreement about the date of this book. They suggest dates ranging over four hundred years. Joel may be among the very earliest of the writing prophets or among the very last; but because his book is placed early among the twelve minor prophets, we shall suppose that he served around 800 B.C.

Joel's name, which was frequent among the Israelites, means "Jehovah is God." His ministry was carried on in the southern kingdom, where his task was to warn the people of the coming judgment of the Lord. The first chapter tells of a great invasion of locusts. The second chapter expands this description. Then 2:18 tells us that the Lord will take pity on his people. Verse 28 begins a dramatic change. The prophet is no longer looking to relief from the locust plague; instead he sees the day of the Lord coming in a fuller sense. This new age will begin when the Lord pours out His Spirit on all flesh. This will be followed by cosmic wonders. Just when these things will occur we cannot be sure, but on the Day of Pentecost Peter quoted Joel to indicate that the new age was beginning (Acts 2:17-21).

B. Hosea (about 750—730 B.C.)

Hosea ministered during the reigns of Uzziah, Jotham, Ahaz, and Hezekiah of Judah, and Jeroboam II of Israel. At that time Assyria was beginning once more to seriously threaten Israel. Israel had fallen into apostasy, and God was preparing to punish her. Hosea's task was to warn the people of this impending doom.

To make this point, Hosea was commanded by God to live out a poignant object lesson. God ordered him to marry a woman, Gomer, from the adulterous population. To this marriage three children were born, and each was given a name that had prophetic significance. Then, as most students understand the story, Gomer abandoned husband and children in her search for pleasure. But hard times eventually befell her; and she was sold into slavery. Hosea was then commanded to purchase Gomer and restore her to his household. So he bought her, and even wrote the price into the record (Hosea 3).

Hosea's domestic tragedy served as an object lesson for Israel. She had proved unfaithful to God, yet He had never ceased to love her. Just as Hosea redeemed Gomer after she had fallen into slavery, so God stood ready to redeem Israel even though she had fallen into spiritual slavery. Hosea had the thankless task of bringing a message of doom to his people. Yet he also brought a message of hope if Israel would only repent.

C. Jonah (about 790 B.C.)

According to 2 Kings 14:25 Jonah was a prophet from Gath Hepher who predicted that the boundaries of Israel would be restored to their former extent. Beyond this we know little about him except what is told in the book of Jonah.

The story of Jonah is one of the most familiar in the Old Testament. God told him to go to Nineveh, the capital of Assyria, and preach repentance. For a patriotic Israelite whose nation had felt the wrath of the Assyrians, this was too much. And so he bought a ticket to Tarshish in what is now Spain, as far from Nineveh as he knew how to go. But God thwarted his escape by sending a storm upon the ship. To save the ship, Jonah was thrown into the sea; but God prepared a "great fish" that swallowed Jonah and later regurgitated him onto dry land.

Following this experience Jonah went to Nineveh and brought the message God had ordered: "Forty more days and Nineveh will be destroyed." Then he sat back and waited for the fireworks, smugly anticipating the destruction of the hated enemy. But the people of Nineveh, from the king on down, repented; and so God withheld His judgment.

Jonah was angered by this and began to pout. God then proceeded to teach him another lesson by giving him a plant to protect him from the heat. Then God caused the plant to wither. When Jonah began to complain, God showed the prophet how contradictory his behavior was. He had been guilty of showing greater concern for a plant than he had for thousands of men, women, children, and "many cattle" in the city of Nineveh.

The message of Jonah speaks so strikingly to the narrow nationalism, racism, and selfishness of our day that we need not elaborate upon it.

D. Amos (about 760 B.C.)

Amos, a shepherd from Judah, carried on his ministry in Israel during the latter years of the reign of Jeroboam II. It was a time of increasing wealth for the northern kingdom, but it was also a time of increasing corruption and oppression of the poor. The book of Amos falls into three parts.

The first part (chapters 1 and 2) pronounces judgment upon Israel's neighbors—Damascus, Philistia, Phoenicia, Edom, Ammon, Moab, and Judah—and then upon Israel herself. The second part (3:1—9:10) concentrates on Israel. Many of their sins— the oppression of the poor, wasteful and luxurious living, empty religious activity—sound painfully contemporary. The final part of the book (9:11-15) brings hope to the people as Amos foresees a wonderful restoration.

E. Isaiah (about 740-690 B.C.)

Isaiah, who must rank as the greatest of the Old Testament writing prophets, carried on a ministry in Judah for a half a century or more from the time of Uzziah to the reign of Manasseh. He lived during the turbulent times when Assyria destroyed the northern kingdom and seriously threatened Judah. As a member of the royal family, he provided counsel, criticism, and hope to several kings of Judah.

The first part of the book (chapters 1—35) brings prophecies of judgment against Judah, Israel, and the surrounding Gentile nations. Chapters 36-39 deal with some of the crucial events that occurred during the reign of Hezekiah. Then chapters 40-66 contain some of the most comforting prophecies of hope to be found anywhere in the Old Testament. Some of these prophecies look to the return of the exiles from captivity, while others look to the coming Messianic kingdom.

Because Isaiah contains so many references to the Messiah, he is sometimes referred to as the "fifth gospel." To cite only a few of these, he prophesied the virgin birth of our Lord (7:14), the glory of His reign (9:6, 7), and his vicarious suffering on the cross (53).

F. Micah (about 740-700 B.C.)

Micah was a younger contemporary of Isaiah, who, though he lived in Judah, addressed his message to both Judah and Israel. Like the other eighth-century prophets—Isaiah, Hosea, and

Amos—he condemned the sins of his day (chapters 1, 2). He especially condemned the oppression of the poor by the rich. For these sins God's judgment would fall upon both Israel and Judah.

The second part of the book (3:1—5:15) looks forward to a coming Messianic kingdom, a kingdom of peace and prosperity. The concluding portion of the book (6:1—7:20) reads as if God were arguing a court case against His people. The indictment against them is devastating as the Lord points out all the ways He has blessed them; yet they have turned away from Him time and time again. But in spite of these charges, Micah's message is not without hope. God would "again have compassion" on them, hurl their "iniquities into the depths of the sea," and "show mercy to Abraham" (7:19, 20).

A number of passages from Micah are considered Messianic. Perhaps the best known of these is found in 5:2, which predicted that the Messiah would be born in Bethlehem.

II. Prophets of the Babylonian Period (612-587 B.C.)

A. Jeremiah (about 626-580 B.C.)

Jeremiah, a sensitive and patriotic man, was called to minister during years when Judah was going into captivity in Babylon. He was not a detached observer of the tragic events; and because his personal life was so interwoven with the life of the nation, we know more about him personally than we do about most of the other prophets.

He was called while he was a young man and felt keenly his inadequacies. His early ministry came during the reign of Josiah, as that good king sought to bring about sweeping reforms. Yet these reforms, pushed more earnestly when a copy of the law was discovered in 621 B.C., did not really reach the hearts of the people. Reformation evaporated following Josiah's untimely death.

The Babylonian power loomed on the horizon, and Jeremiah had to deliver a message of God's judgment upon his nation. It was a message he dreaded to bring; but when he tried to suppress it, God's word was like a burning fire, shut up in his bones (20:9). As he said defeat was sure and encouraged surrender to the Babylonians, the anger of the people and the leaders was aroused against him. He was threatened, plotted against, and imprisoned. On one occasion Jeremiah dictated his prophecies to his faithful scribe, Baruch, and had them delivered to King Jehoiakim. The

106

king arrogantly cut up the scroll and burned it. Undeterrred by the king's action, Jeremiah dictated another scroll to Baruch (chapter 36).

Nebuchadnezzar finally captured Jerusalem in 586 B.C. He took many of the people to Babylon, but left some to till the soil. Jeremiah was released from prison and allowed to accompany the governor, Gedaliah, to Mizpah. Then die-hards assassinated Gedaliah and took refuge with the Ammonites. The remaining men of Judah were afraid Nebuchadnezzar would take revenge by slaughtering them all. They fled to Egypt, taking the reluctant Jeremiah with them. There the prophet spent the rest of his days.

Jeremiah has become known as the "weeping prophet," and the title seems most appropriate. In the book of Lamentations he bewails the fate of Jerusalem. The book is one continuous cry of anguish, with scarcely a glimmer of hope.

Yet Jeremiah was not completely without hope. He foretold a new covenant in which the sins of his people would be forgiven (31:31-34). Christ brought that covenant, and by it we are freed from sin.

B. Nahum (about 615 B.C.)

Nahum confines his book to one theme—the overthrow of the hated Nineveh. Since Nineveh fell to a combined force of Babylonians and Medes in 612 B.C., it would appear that Nahum wrote a short time before this event. We suggest the year 615, but it may have been as much as thirty or forty years earlier. The destruction of Nineveh was presented by Nahum as a just recompense for its cruelty against the nations it conquered.

C. Zephaniah (about 630 B.C.)

Zephaniah prophesied during the reign of Josiah, but probably before his great reforms took effect. Zephaniah portrayed the doom that awaited Judah because she had turned to the worship of Baal, Moloch, and "the starry hosts" (1:4-6).

God's judgment would rest on Judah (chapter 1) as well as on the nations all about—the Philistines, the Moabites, the Ammonites, the Cushites, the Assyrians (chapter 2). Yet even these dire predictions did not end without hope, for the closing verses of the book (3:9-20) look forward to the restoration of a faithful remnant. "At that time I will gather you; and at that time I will bring you home" (3:20).

D. Habakkuk (about 610 B.C.)

Habakkuk, who lived just before the invasion of the Babylonians (Chaldeans), had a problem. Wicked Jews were persecuting righteous Jews, and to troubled Habakkuk it seemed that God was unaware of it or didn't care. When the prophet complained of this, God assured him that the answer was already on the way in the form of the Babylonians, who would punish the wicked Jews.

But to Habakkuk, a good patriotic Jew, this was worse than no answer. In his mind the most wicked Jew was better than the Babylonians. Habakkuk complained even more bitterly. Then God's answer came: "The righteous will live by his faith" (2:4). In other words, the righteous will not always be able to understand God's ways, and so he must accept God's actions by faith.

This verse was later used by Paul as the keystone in his great theological work, the book of Romans (Romans 1:17). This verse in turn became the basis for Martin Luther's revolt against the Roman Catholic Church.

III. Prophets of the Exile (586-538 B.C.)

A. Ezekiel (about 597-570 B.C.)

Ezekiel was carried away to Babylon by the forces of Nebuchadnezzar in 597 B.C. His first mission was to counter the message of the false prophets who were predicting an early return of the exiles. Then after the fall of Jerusalem, his task was to bring a message of hope to the discouraged people.

Perhaps the two best-known passages in the book are his assertion of personal responsibility—"The soul who sins is the one who will die" (18:4)—and his vision of the valley of dry bones (37:1-14). This vision was a message of hope to a people who desperately needed it. The dry bones of their destroyed nation would receive new life.

B. Obadiah (about 840 B.C.—580 B.C.)

Scholars debate the date of this shortest book in the Old Testament. It may have come as early as Jehoram's reign (848-841 B.C.) or following the destruction of Jerusalem in 586 B.C. Its message pronounces God's judgment upon Edom for their support of Jerusalem's enemies. That judgment was eventually carried out. Edom's fabulous fortress city, Petra, is now a tourist attraction but not a living city. Obadiah ends on a triumphant note: "The kingdom will be the Lord's."

C. Daniel (605-530 B.C.)

Daniel was taken to Babylonia by Nebuchadnezzar as a hostage in 606 B.C. He was one of the most remarkable persons in the Old Testament. Because of his ability and God's blessings, he became a trusted advisor to Nebuchadnezzar and Belshazzar, and in the Persian period to Darius and Cyrus. Even though his ministry was almost exclusively to Gentiles rather than to his own people, his piety and wisdom became legendary in his own lifetime.

The first six chapters of the book cover his activities among the Babylonians and Persians. Chapters 7 through 12 contain a series of visions that encompass the whole sweep of human history from Daniel's own time until the Lord's return. Our Lord referred to Daniel in His great prophetic discourse (Matthew 24:15). Scholars differ in their interpretation of the last six chapters of Daniel, but all acknowledge that one must take this Old Testament book into account in attempting to interpret the prophecies of the New Testament.

IV. Prophets of the Post-Exilic Period (538-431 B.C.)

A. Haggai (520 B.C.)

When the exiles returned to Judah, they built an altar and soon laid the foundations to rebuild the temple. But they became discouraged, and the work stopped. Haggai's mission was to encourage the people to take up this task again. His word brought results. The work was renewed, and four years later the second temple was completed.

B. Zechariah (520-518 B.C.)

Zechariah was a contemporary of Haggai and shared with him in his mission to encourage a renewed effort to rebuild the temple. But much of Zechariah's book is a good example of prophetic literature that looks to a future fulfillment. Some of his prophecies refer to Christ. He is to be a priest-king (6:13); His triumphal entry is predicted (9:9); His crucifixion is mentioned (12:10); and His ultimate victory is foretold (chapter 14).

C. Malachi (431 B.C.)

Little is known about the author of the last book in the Old Testament, but from the contents we conclude that he lived and prophesied after the time of Ezra and Nehemiah. He brings a message of warning to the priests for their carelessness, and to the people for their unfaithfulness and worldliness. The book concludes with the prediction that Elijah would return before that "great and dreadful day of the Lord" (4:5). After a wait of more than four hundred years this prophecy was fulfilled in the person of John the Baptist (Matthew 11:7-15).

Some of the Prophecies
Fulfilled in Jesus

Psalm 132:11	Heir of David	Luke 1:26-33
Isaiah 7:14	Virgin Birth	Matthew 1:22, 23
Micah 5:2	Birth in Bethlehem	Matthew 2:1-6
Hosea 11:1	Stay in Egypt	Matthew 2:14, 15
Jeremiah 31:15	Mourning in Bethlehem	Matthew 2:16-18
Isaiah 9:1, 2	Home in Galilee	Matthew 2:21, 22
Isaiah 53:4	Healing Ministry	Matthew 8:16, 17
Isaiah 6:9, 10	Lack of Understanding	Matthew 13:10-15
Psalm 78:2	Teaching in Parables	Matthew 13:34, 35
Zechariah 9:9	Triumphal Entry	Matthew 21:1-9
Isaiah 53:1; 6:10	Disbelief	John 12:37-41
Psalm 69:4	Unreasoning Hatred	John 15:23-25
Psalm 42:9	Defection of Judas	John 13:18
Isaiah 53:12	Numbered With Transgressors	Luke 22:37
Psalm 22:18	Clothing Divided by Lot	John 19:23, 24
Psalm 69:21	Vinegar to drink	John 19:28, 29
Psalm 34:20	No Broken Bones	John 19:31-37
Zechariah 12:10	Pierced by Spear	John 9:31-37
Isaiah 53:9	With the Rich in Death	Matthew 27:57-60
Psalm 16:8-11	Resurrection	Acts 2:24-32
Psalm 110:1	Seated on God's Right Hand	Mark 16:19
Amos 9:11, 12	Mission to Gentiles	Acts 15:13-18